PRACTICE – ASSESS – DIAGNOSE

180 Days of HIGH-FREQUENCY WORDS for Second Grade

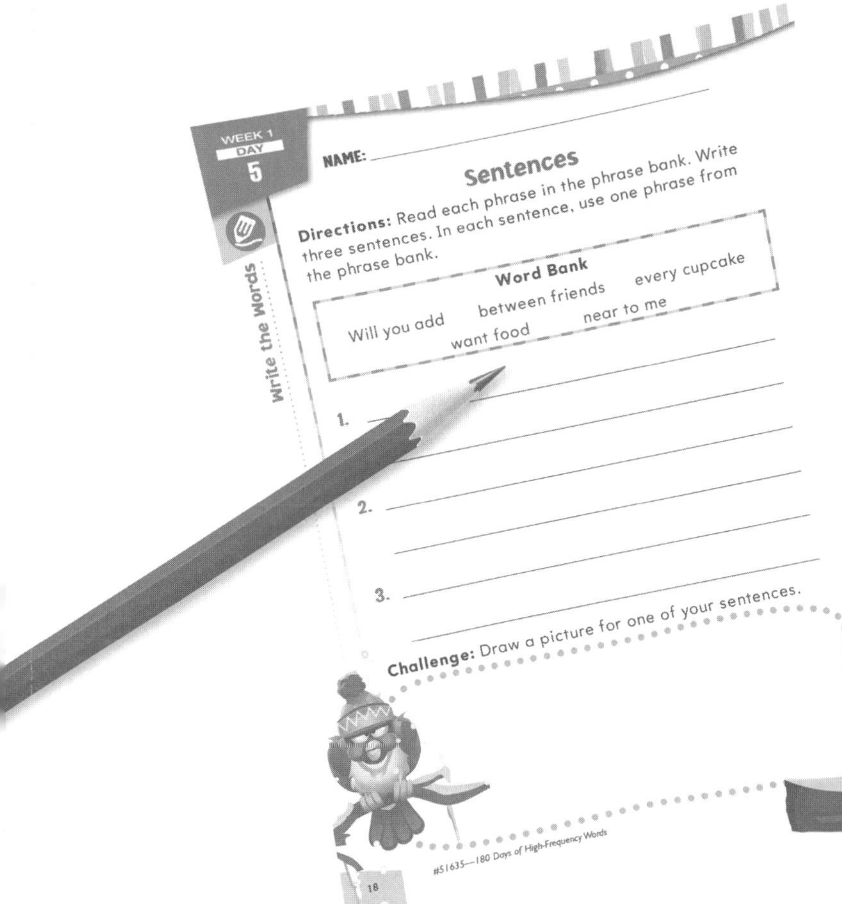

Author
Adair Solomon, M.A.T.

SHELL EDUCATION

For information on how this resource meets national and other state standards, see page 4. You may also review this information by visiting our website at www.teachercreatedmaterials.com/administrators/correlations/ and following the on-screen directions.

Publishing Credits

Corinne Burton, M.A.Ed., *Publisher*; Conni Medina, M.A.Ed., *Managing Editor*; Emily R. Smith, M.A.Ed., *Content Director*; Angela Johnson, M.A.Ed., M.F.A., *Editor*; Lee Aucoin, *Senior Multimedia Designer*; Don Tran, *Production Artist;* Kyleena Harper, *Assistant Editor*

Image Credits

All images from iStock and Shutterstock.

Standards

Shell Education
A division of Teacher Created Materials
5301 Oceanus Drive
Huntington Beach, CA 92649-1030

http://www.tcmpub.com/shell-education

ISBN 978-1-4258-1635-3

Printed by: 51497
Printed in: Taiwan

TABLE OF CONTENTS

INTRODUCTION AND RESEARCH

If you teach early learners to read, you know how important the mastery of high-frequency words is to reading success. Students who are exposed to and learn high-frequency words during these critical years of academia set the foundation for reading and overall success as scholars. The words in this book make up "65% of written material" that we encounter on a daily basis and are the connective tissues used to craft even the simplest written sentence (Fry 2000, 4).

The Need for Practice

To be successful in today's classroom, students must be able to accurately identify and read high-frequency words. Building accuracy and fluency when reading these words is critical for later reading success mainly because, unlike other words, "some of these often-used words do not follow regular phonics rules" (Fry 2000, 4). Being able to read these words allows students to focus on fluency instead of decoding while reading. The National Reading Panel suggests that repeated exposure to high-frequency words is crucial to reading instruction and sets the building blocks for decoding, fluency, and comprehension (2000). According to Robert Marzano, "practice has always been, and always will be, a necessary ingredient to learning procedural knowledge at a level at which students execute it independently" (2010, 83).

Understanding Assessment

In addition to providing opportunities for frequent practice, teachers must be able to assess students' acquisition of high-frequency words. This is important for teachers to adequately support students' progress in fluency and comprehension. Assessment is a long-term process that often involves careful analysis of students' responses from discussions, projects, practice sheets, and tests. In short, the data gathered from assessments should be used to inform instruction: slow down, speed up, or reteach. This type of evaluation is called *formative assessment* (McIntosh 1997).

HOW TO USE THIS BOOK

180 Days of High-Frequency Words for Second Grade offers weekly units to guide students as they practice and learn words every day of the school year. Each daily activity is designed to engage students with the words of the week. On the first day, students are introduced to the words of the week. For the rest of the week, students complete activities in which they must **recognize**, **play with**, **use**, and **write** the words of the week.

Easy to Use and Standards Based

The Every Student Succeeds Act (ESSA) mandates that all states adopt challenging academic standards that help students meet the goal of college and career readiness. While many states already adopted academic standards prior to ESSA, the act continues to hold states accountable for detailed and comprehensive standards. These daily activities reinforce grade-level skills and allow students to read, write, speak, and listen to high-frequency words every day of the school year. This chart indicates reading, writing, language, and print concept standards that are addressed throughout this book.

Reading—phonics and word recognition	Read common high-frequency words by sight.
	Distinguish between similarly spelled words by identifying the sounds of the letters that differ.
	Add drawings or other visual displays to descriptions as desired to provide additional detail.
Writing—text type and purpose	Use a combination of drawing, dictating, and writing to compose informative/explanatory texts in which students name what they are writing about and supply some information about the topic.
Language—conventions of standard English	Demonstrate command of the conventions of standard English grammar and usage when writing or speaking.
	Print many uppercase and lowercase letters.
	Use frequently occurring nouns and verbs.
	Produce and expand complete sentences in shared language activities.
	Demonstrate command of the conventions of standard English capitalization, punctuation, and spelling when writing.
	Capitalize the first word.
	Spell simple words phonetically, drawing on knowledge of sound-letter relationships.
Print concepts	Demonstrate understanding of the organization and basic features of print.
	Follow words from left to right, top to bottom, and page by page.
	Recognize that spoken words are represented in written language by specific sequences of letters.
	Understand that words are separated by spaces in print.

HOW TO USE THIS BOOK *(cont.)*

Using the Practice Pages

Practice pages provide instruction for each day of the school year. Teachers may wish to prepare packets of weekly practice pages for the classroom or for homework. As outlined on page 4, every page is aligned to phonics skills and word recognition skills.

The week starts with introductory activities. The focus for the first half of the week is to familiarize students with the words of the week.

Each day of the week focuses on a new skill. There are five overarching skills used in this book: introducing, recognizing, playing, using, and writing with the words. See page 7 for detailed objectives for each day.

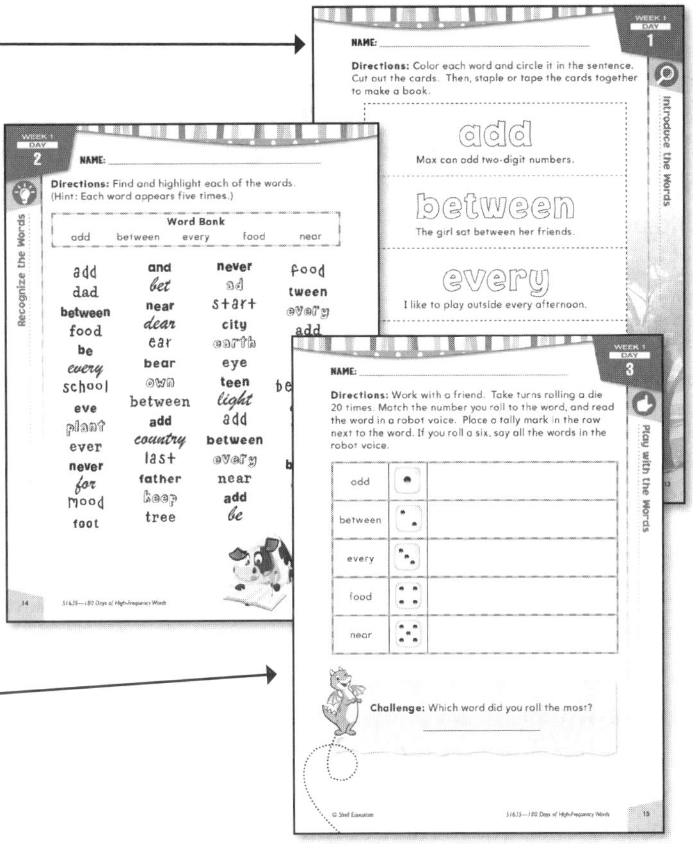

Each week students explore new words through kinesthetic activities.

At the end of the week, students read and write using the high-frequency words of the week. For a detailed explanation of each activity, see pages 8–9.

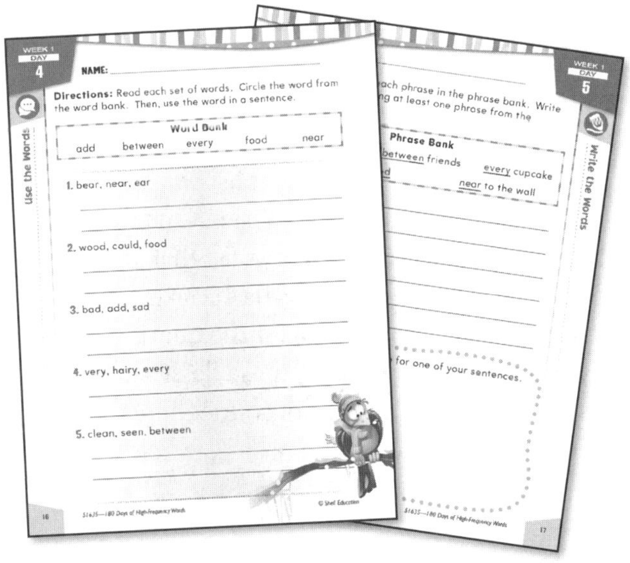

HOW TO USE THIS BOOK *(cont.)*

Using the Resources

The student extension activities, assessment materials, and flash cards in this book are available as digital PDFs and Microsoft Word® documents online. A complete list of the available documents is provided on page 216. To access the Digital Resources, go to: www.tcmpub.com/download-files. Enter this code: 86086829. Follow the on-screen directions.

The quarterly assessment tools will aid the classroom teacher in tracking the high-frequency words your class recognizes throughout the year. The checklist on page 11 should be reproduced for each student in the class. Use it to record the words students recognize each quarter. Use page 12 to log students' progress throughout the year. This page can be used to see, at a glance, common high-frequency words that still need additional practice, as well as trends to drive whole-class instruction.

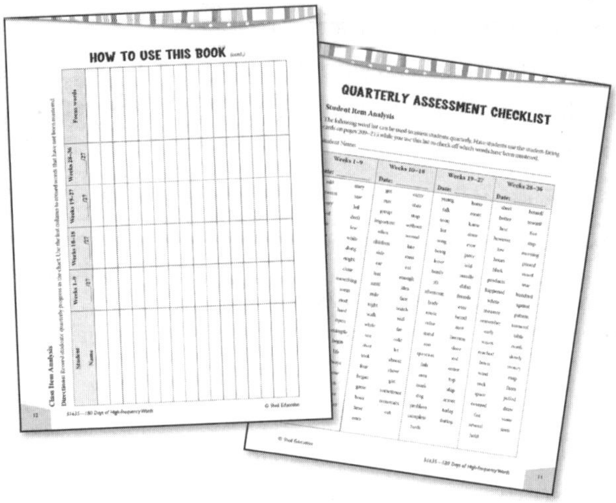

Pages 199–206 can be used for home/school connection extension activities. The games and suggestions are engaging and will help students practice reading and identifying all of the high-frequency words in this book.

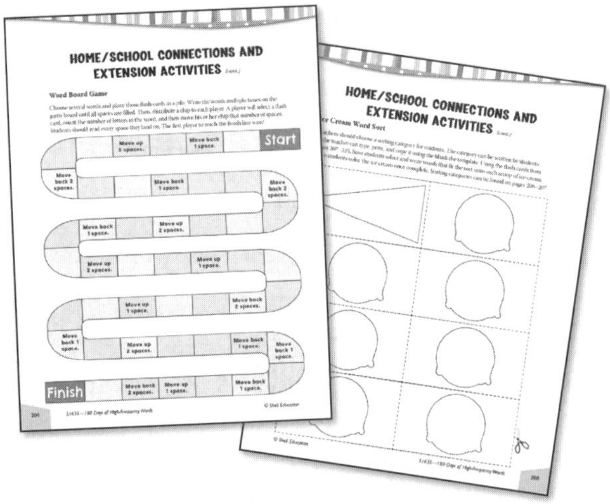

Dr. Edward Fry created a list of 1,000 Instant Words to teach children. That list was used in choosing the words for this series. On pages 209–215, the words from Fry's list that are used in this book are provided as flash cards. These cards can be used as a tool for the quarterly assessments. Additionally, these flash cards can used with the home/school connection and extension activities.

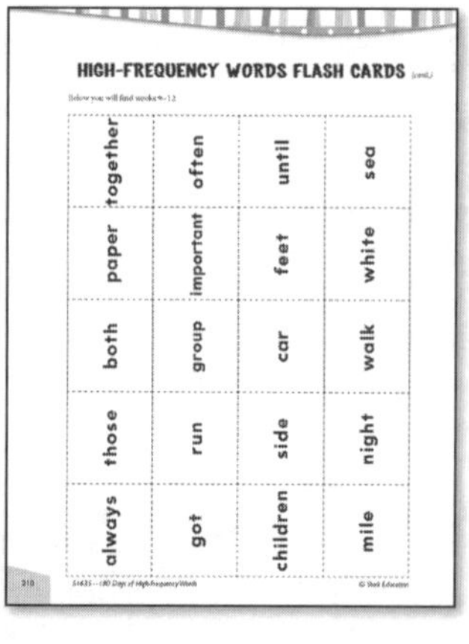

HOW TO USE THIS BOOK *(cont.)*

For 180 days, educators can use this book to support students' acquisition and recognition of high-frequency words. The book is divided into 36 weeks, with five days of activities per week. Each week, students are introduced to three high-frequency words. The format of the week is as follows: introduce the words, recognize the words, play with the words, use the words, and write the words.

Below is a list of daily activities. Detailed descriptions for each activity can be found on pages 8–9.

Daily Description	Names of Activities
Day 1—Introduce the Words For the first day of each week, students complete introductory activities. These activities are designed to introduce and familiarize students with the high-frequency words of the week. Students create flash cards with the high-frequency words. These can be stored in a zip-top bag at each student's desk or taken home as a study tool for the week.	Highlight Book Mastery Folder Picture Ring Ringer Word Book Word Write
Day 2—Recognize the Words The second day of each week is devoted to recognition activities. Activities are designed around identifying the high-frequency words of the week.	ABC Hidden Words (First Half of the Year) Hidden Words (Second Half of the Year) Scrambled Words Triplets Word Shapes
Day 3—Play with the Words On day three, students play with the words of the week. These activities are geared toward tactile manipulation of the high-frequency words. These activities infuse play, art, and hands-on activities for the week.	Color by Word Memory Game Roy G. Biv Telephone Words Word Mix Up Word Race Word Tiles
Day 4—Use the Words On the fourth day of the week, students use the words of the week in context. Students tell or write stories using the words, or act as word detectives and read the words.	Best Word Definitions Missing Words Silly Sentences Story Words The Best
Day 5—Write the Words On day five, students engage in writing activities. Using the high-frequency words of the week, students craft stories and illustrations. These activities motivate all students to apply what they have learned during the week.	Building Sentences Captions Picture It Picture Prompt Sentences

HOW TO USE THIS BOOK *(cont.)*

Below is a detailed explanation and rationale for each activity in 180 Days of *High-Frequency Words for Second Grade.*

Activity	Description
ABC	Students write the high-frequency words in alphabetical order. Then, they write the high-frequency words in reverse alphabetical order.
Best Word	Students scan three words and circle the high-frequency words. Then, they create sentences using the words.
Building Sentences	Students read the words in the word banks and the phrases in the phrase banks. Then, they create three sentences including at least one word and one phrase.
Captions	Students look at pictures. Next, they write three sentences that represent the pictures. Challenge: Students draw stars next to the sentences that include the most high-frequency words.
Color by Word	Students look at the pictures and codes. They use these codes to color in the images on the activity pages.
Hidden Words (First Half of the Year)	Students read the high-frequency words, then find and circle them in word puzzles. Each word of the week is in each puzzle one time.
Hidden Words (Second Half of the Year)	Students read the high-frequency words, then write the words twice (vertically and horizontally) using the provided grid paper. Next, they fill in the blanks with random letters. Then, students cut their puzzles out and give them to friends to solve.
Highlight Book	Students read sentences and highlight the high-frequency words. Then, they write the words on the lines below. Next, they cut out the word cards and create practice booklets using tape or staples.
Mastery Folder	Students write each high-frequency word one time. Next, they color the words on the flash cards and then cut them out. Cards can be placed in students' folders and practiced throughout the week.
Memory Game	This activity can be played individually or with a partner. Students cut out high-frequency word cards, then place them facedown on any hard surface. Next, a student flips one card and says the revealed word. Then, the student flips another card and says the word. If the cards match, they stay face up. If the cards don't match, they are turned facedown again. Students try to get all the cards to face up.
Missing Words	Students read cloze sentences, then determine the correct high-frequency words to complete the sentences. Then, they fill in the blanks with correct words.
Picture It	A student creates one sentence that includes at least three of the high-frequency words from the word bank. Then, the student draws a picture that represents the sentence.
Picture Prompt	Students look at the pictures and visualize they are in them. Then, they write short stories that include as many high-frequency words as possible. Challenge: Students read the stories and highlight the high-frequency words.
Picture Ring	Students write the high-frequency words. Then, they look at pictures and write the high-frequency words that correspond with the pictures. Finally, they cut out the word cards, punch holes in the cards, and place them on binder rings.

HOW TO USE THIS BOOK *(cont.)*

Activity	Description
Ringer	Students trace the high-frequency words, then circle the words in the accompanying sentences. Next, they cut out the word cards, punch holes in the cards, and place them on binder rings. Throughout the year, students add words to their rings and use the cards for practice.
Roy G. Biv	Students trace around high-frequency words using the sequential colors of the rainbow: red, orange, yellow, green, blue, and violet.
Scrambled Words	Students locate and circle the high-frequency words that are hidden in a string of letters. Then, they unscramble the high-frequency words and write them correctly.
Sentences	Students read the word phrases in the phrase banks. Then, they create three sentences using the phrases. Challenge: Students draw pictures of one of their sentences.
Silly Sentences	Students read the beginning of sentences and circle the high-frequency words. Then, they use their imagination to complete sentences with silly endings.
Story Words	Students read cloze paragraphs and determine the correct high-frequency words to complete them. Then, students fill in the blanks with their chosen words. Challenge: Students record the words they used the most.
Telephone Words	Students write the high-frequency words. Next, they use the telephone pad graphic to determine the value of the letters within the high-frequency words and record them in the spaces provided. Then, they add the numbers together to find the sum of each word. Challenge: Students record the word with the highest value.
The Best	Students read pairs of sentences and highlight the high-frequency words. Then, they compare the sentences and draw stars next to the one that makes sense.
Triplets	Students write high-frequency words three times using different colors.
Word Book	Students color in high-frequency words, then circle the words in the accompanying sentences. Then, they cut out the word cards and create practice booklets using tape or staples.
Word Mix Up	Students write high-frequency words forward, then backward. Then, they write high-frequency words in uppercase, then lowercase.
Word Race	A die is needed to complete this activity, and can be played alone or with a partner. Students roll the die and match the roll to the corresponding word on the page. Next, they say the word in a voice determined in the directions. Then, they place an X in the row next to the word. There are enough spaces to play at least 10 rounds. Challenge: Students record the word they rolled the most.
Word Shapes	Students draw geometric shapes around specific high-frequency words. Challenge: Students write the high-frequency words using unique, fun fonts of their own.
Word Tiles	Students cut out the letters. Next, they create the high-frequency words with the letters. Then, they glue the words onto the page.
Word Write	Students read the high-frequency words in the word banks. Next, they look at pictures with accompanying sentences. They read each sentence and circle the high-frequency word. Then, they write the high-frequency word on the line below.

HOW TO USE THIS BOOK *(cont.)*

Diagnostic Quarterly Assessment

Teachers can use the *Student Item Analysis Checklist* to monitor students' learning. This tool can enable teachers or parents to quickly score students' work and monitor students' progress. Teachers and parents can see which high-frequency words students know and which ones they do not.

The words in this book are divided into four list. Each list can be used to assess students quarterly throughout the year. The *Student Item Analysis Checklist* on page 11 should be used by the teacher to administer the assessment. The *High-Frequency Word Flash Cards* on pages 207–215 should be used as the student-facing list. Below you will find detailed steps to administer each component of the diagnostic assessment.

To Complete the Student Item Analysis Checklist:

- Write or type the student's name on the name line at the top of the chart. One copy per student is needed to track his or her ongoing progress throughout the year.
- Give each student the flash cards that correspond with the *Student Item Analysis Checklist* on page 11. Use the *Student Item Analysis Checklist* to mark students' responses. Students should be able to identify each word in a few seconds.
- The numbers across the top of the chart can be used to log each student's percentage of correct words in each quarter of the school year. For each quarter, record how many high-frequency words each student is able to accurately identify.

To Complete the Class Item Analysis:

- After each student has completed a list from the *Student Item Analysis Checklist,* use the *Class Item Analysis* chart on page 12 to log the results. Write or type students' names in the far-left column. Depending on the number of students in your class, more than one copy of the form may be needed, or you may need to add rows.
- Indicated across the top of the chart are the weeks that correspond with each word list. Students are assessed every 9 weeks.
- For each student, record his or her score in the appropriate column.
- Students' scores can be placed in the middle columns and scored by averaging the number of words in the week compared to the words identified correctly. Place the results in the correct column. Use these scores as benchmarks to determine how students are performing. This allows for four benchmark assessments during the year that can be used to gather formative diagnostic data. Use the last column to identify trends in the classroom for additional high-frequency lesson planning.

HOW TO USE THIS BOOK *(cont.)*

Student Item Analysis

The following word list can be used to assess students quarterly. Have students use the student-facing cards on pages 209–215 while you use this list to check off which words have been mastered.

Student Name: ______________________________

Weeks 1–9		Weeks 10–18		Weeks 19–27		Weeks 28–36	
_____/45		_____/45		_____/45		_____/45	
Date: __________		Date: __________		Date: __________		Date: __________	
add	story	got	carry	young	horse	short	himself
between	saw	run	state	talk	room	better	toward
every	left	group	stop	soon	knew	best	five
food	don't	important	without	list	since	however	step
near	few	often	second	song	ever	low	morning
own	while	children	late	being	piece	hours	passed
below	along	side	miss	leave	told	black	vowel
country	might	car	eat	family	usually	products	true
plant	close	feet	enough	it's	didn't	happened	hundred
last	something	until	idea	afternoon	friends	whole	against
school	seem	mile	face	body	easy	measure	pattern
father	next	night	watch	music	heard	remember	numeral
keep	hard	walk	real	color	sure	early	table
tree	open	white	far	stand	become	waves	north
never	example	sea	cold	sun	door	reached	slowly
start	begin	river	let	question	red	listen	money
city	life	took	almost	fish	order	wind	map
earth	always	four	above	area	top	rock	farm
eye	those	began	girl	mark	ship	space	pulled
light	both	grow	sometimes	dog	across	covered	draw
thought	paper	book	mountain	problem	today	fast	voice
head	together	hear	cut	complete	during	several	seen
under		once		birds		hold	

Class Item Analysis

Directions: Record students' quarterly progress in the chart. Use the last column to record words that have not been mastered.

Student Name	Weeks 1–9 Date: _____	Weeks 10–18 Date: _____	Weeks 19–27 Date: _____	Weeks 28–36 Date: _____	Focus words

NAME: ______________________________

Directions: Color each word, and circle it in the sentence. Cut out the cards. Then, staple or tape the cards together to make a book.

add

Max can add two-digit numbers.

between

The girl sat between her friends.

every

I like to play outside every afternoon.

food

Amy put the food in her lunchbox.

near

The dog is near the door.

NAME: ______________________________

Directions: Find and highlight each of the words. (Hint: Each word appears five times.)

Word Bank

add between every food near

add	and	never	food
dad	bet	ad	tween
between	near	start	every
food	dear	city	add
be	ear	earth	food
every	bear	eye	near
school	own	teen	between
eve	between	light	every
plant	add	add	food
ever	country	between	near
never	last	every	between
for	father	near	every
mood	keep	add	food
foot	tree	be	near

NAME: ______________________________

Directions: Work with a friend. Take turns rolling a die 20 times. Match the number you roll to the word, and read the word in a *robot voice*. Place a tally mark in the row next to the word. If you roll a six, say all the words in the robot voice.

add		
between	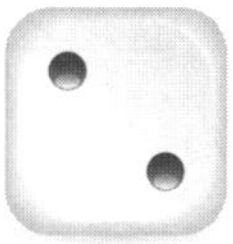	
every	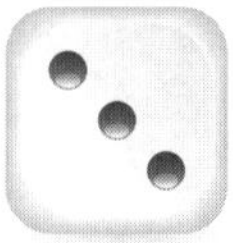	
food		
near		

Challenge: Which word did you roll the most?

____

NAME: ______________________________

Directions: Read each set of words. Circle the word from the word bank. Then, use the word in a sentence.

Word Bank				
add	between	every	food	near

1. bear, near, ear

____

____

2. wood, could, food

____

____

3. bad, add, sad

____

____

4. very, hairy, every

____

____

5. clean, seen, between

____

____

NAME: ____

Directions: Read each phrase in the phrase bank. Write three sentences using at least one phrase in each from the phrase bank.

Phrase Bank

can you add	between friends	every cupcake
smell the food		near to the wall

1. ____

____

2. ____

____

3. ____

____

Challenge: Draw a picture for one of your sentences.

Introduce the Words

NAME: ______________________________

Directions: Color each word, then circle that word in the sentence. Cut along the dotted lines to make word cards. Punch a hole in each card and place it on a practice ring.

own

I have my own bedroom.

below

The plane flew below the clouds.

country

My best friend lives in a small country.

plant

Will you help me plant the flowers?

last

The last person in line will close the classroom door.

NAME: ____

Directions: Read the words in the word bank. Then, find and circle them in the puzzle.

Word Bank

own below country plant last

W T W L W Y T

V O W O T R C

B M L N R T T

K E A C S N S

B L G B D U A

P R G S R O L

B N W O I C W

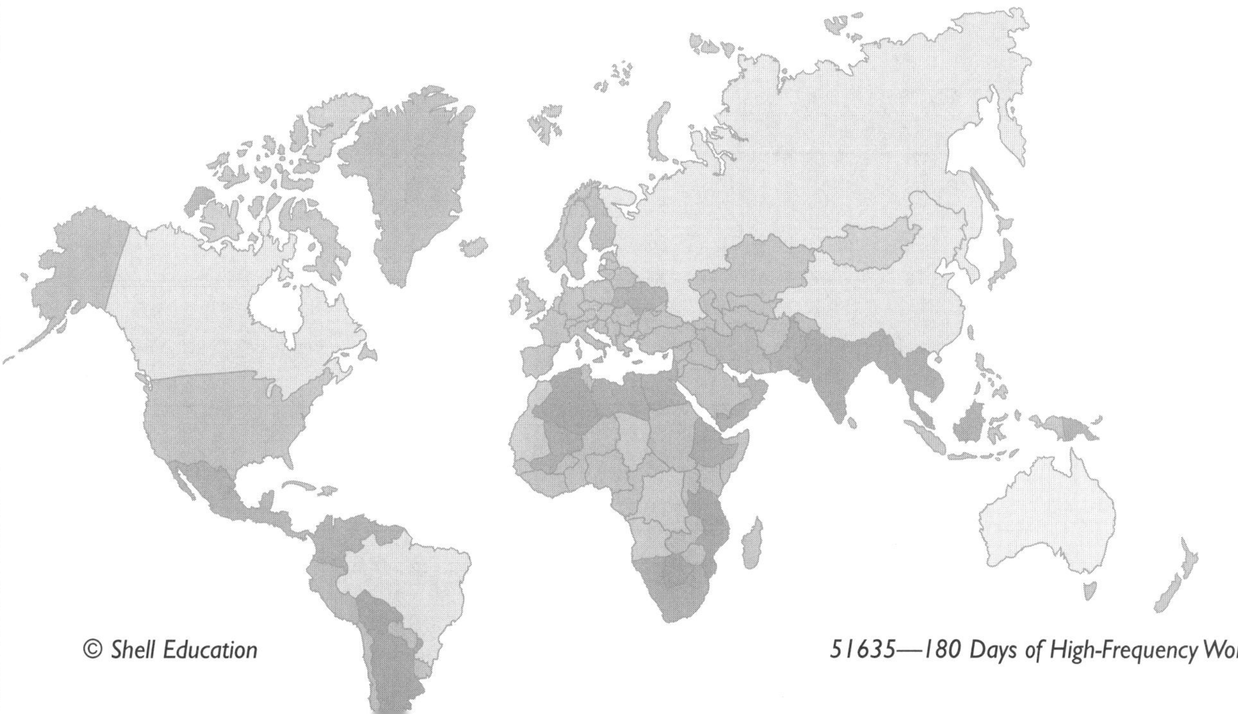

Play with the Words

NAME: ____________________

Directions: Write each word. Then, write the word backward.

example: boy yob

1. own ____________ ____________
2. below ____________ ____________
3. country ____________ ____________
4. plant ____________ ____________
5. last ____________ ____________

Directions: Write each word in uppercase letters, then write the word in lowercase letters.

example: BOY boy

1. below ____________ ____________
2. country ____________ ____________
3. own ____________ ____________
4. last ____________ ____________
5. plant ____________ ____________

NAME: ____________________

Directions: Write the correct word from the word bank in the space to complete each sentence. Then, rewrite the sentence on the lines below.

Word Bank				
own	below	country	plant	last

1. My family will ____________ trees in the spring.

   ____

   ____

2. I am going to visit another ____________ this summer.

   ____

   ____

3. Juan can tie his ____________ shoes!

   ____

   ____

4. We walked ____________ the bridge in the park.

   ____

   ____

5. What is your first and ____________ name?

   ____

   ____

NAME: ____________________

Directions: Write a sentence that includes at least three words from the word bank. Then, draw a picture to go with it.

Word Bank				
own	below	country	plant	last

____

____

____

NAME: ______________________________

Directions: Look at each picture, and read the sentence next to it. Circle the word from the word bank in the sentence. Then, write the word on the line.

Word Bank				
school	father	keep	tree	never

	My father wears a tie to work. ______________________________
	Can I keep the cute puppy? ______________________________
	The school is near my house. ______________________________
	The tree was planted, and it began to grow. ______________________________
	David never forgets to brush his teeth. ______________________________

NAME: ______________________________

Recognize the Words

Directions: Find the words from the word bank among the scrambled letters, and circle them. Then, unscramble the letters below to create the words. Write the words three times each.

Word Bank				
school	father	keep	tree	never

dksovalksfatherksdusiajeepsldftreelsdfkaneverk

dkfsokeepidsksldischoolfkdoskneverkofsdkfdls

1. epke ______________________________
2. vreen ______________________________
3. colohs ______________________________
4. rtfhae ______________________________
5. etre ______________________________

NAME: ____

Directions: Color in the words. Then, trace around each word six times to create a rainbow of red, orange, yellow, green, blue, and purple.

father

tree

never

school

keep

Use the Words

NAME: ______________________________

Directions: Read each sentence, and highlight the word from the word bank. Then, compare each sentence pair, and put a star next to the one that makes sense.

Word Bank				
school	father	keep	tree	never

1a. I like to keep my room clean.

1b. The house will keep on the corner.

2a. A school of fish swam in the sea.

2b. A school is where doctors help people.

3a. The fish climbed the tree to get away from the cat.

3b. The tree in my yard fell during the hurricane.

4a. I have to ask my father if I can go to the movie.

4b. Dana can run father than her little brother, Tony.

5a. There are never 70 minutes in an hour.

5b. The sun never rises every morning.

NAME: ____

Directions: Write three sentences about the picture. Use as many words from the word bank as you can in each sentence. Underline the words.

Word Bank

school father keep tree never

1. ____

____

2. ____

____

3. ____

____

Challenge: Draw a star next to the sentence that has the most high-frequency words.

Introduce the Words

NAME: ______________________________

Directions: Color each word, and circle it in the sentence. Cut out the cards. Then, staple or tape the cards together to make a book.

start

Jack was excited to start the first day of school.

city

There are very tall buildings in the city.

earth

We should all plant seeds in the earth every fall.

eye

Ella hurt her left eye when she bumped into the tree.

light

Mom asked Dad to light the candles on the birthday cake.

Recognize the Words

NAME: ______________________________

Directions: Find and highlight each of the words. (Hint: Each word appears five times.)

Word Bank

start city earth eye light

start
city
start
earth
city
star
tart
stat
city
start
city
start
city
sit

tiny
cite
start
earth
eye
earth
earth
bath
wrath
eight
light
eye
light

earth
eye
ear
egg
bye
light
eye
light
eye
light
lite
night
might
school

father
keep
tree
never
thought
head
under
story
saw
left
don't
few
while
along

NAME: ______________________________

Directions: Work with a friend. Take turns rolling a die 10 times. Match the number you roll to the word, and read the word in a funny voice. Place an X in the row next to it. If you roll a six, say all the words.

start		
city	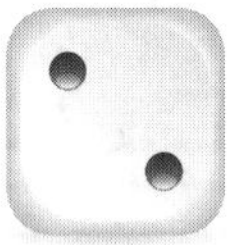	
earth		
eye		
light		

Challenge: Which word did you roll the most?

____

NAME: ______________________________

Directions: Read each set of words. Circle the word from the word bank. Then, use the word in a sentence.

Word Bank				
start	city	earth	eye	light

1. light, long, right

____

____

2. eye, down, most

____

____

3. over, any, city

____

____

4. start, just, old

____

____

5. sound, earth, around

____

____

NAME: ______________________________

Directions: Read each phrase in the phrase bank. Write three sentences using at least one phrase in each from the phrase bank.

Phrase Bank

too soon to start   city by the bay   earth is
eye and nose   light the way

1. ______________________________
____

2. ______________________________
____

3. ______________________________
____

Challenge: Draw a picture for one of your sentences.

NAME: ______________________________

Directions: Color each word, then circle that word in the sentence. Cut along the dotted lines to make word cards. Punch a hole in each card and place it on a practice ring.

thought

I thought the movie was funny.

head

Carter used his head to hit the soccer ball.

under

The cat slept under the chair.

story

Will you read the story again?

saw

He used the saw to cut down the tree.

Recognize the Words

NAME: ______________________________

Directions: Read the words in the word bank. Then, find and circle them in the puzzle.

Word Bank

thought head under story saw

D	U	R	A	F	T	N
A	V	E	A	D	H	F
E	I	D	A	C	G	U
H	R	N	B	C	U	V
P	G	U	R	P	O	B
S	T	O	R	Y	H	E
S	A	W	M	B	T	K

NAME: ______________________________

Directions: Write each word. Then, write the word backward.

example: word drow

1. head ____________ ____________
2. thought ____________ ____________
3. story ____________ ____________
4. under ____________ ____________
5. saw ____________ ____________

Directions: Write each word in uppercase letters, then write the word in lowercase letters.

example: WORD word

1. thought ____________ ____________
2. under ____________ ____________
3. saw ____________ ____________
4. head ____________ ____________
5. story ____________ ____________

Use the Words

NAME: ______________________________

Directions: Write the correct word from the word bank in the space to complete each sentence. Then, rewrite the sentence on the lines below.

Word Bank

thought head under story saw

1. The teacher read the ______________ to the class.

____

____

2. I hit my ______________ on the monkey bars.

____

____

3. At the airport, Kim ______________ the plane land.

____

____

4. She ______________ it was going to rain.

____

____

5. Is the pencil ______________ the chair?

____

____

NAME: ________________________________

Directions: Write a sentence that includes at least three words from the word bank. Then, draw a picture to go with it.

Word Bank

thought head under story saw

____

____

____

NAME: ______________________________

Directions: Look at each picture, and read the sentence next to it. Circle the word from the word bank in the sentence. Then, write the word on the line.

Word Bank				
left	don't	few	while	along

My aunt cooked while I set the table.

____

Don't forget to read your book every day.

____

Do you write with your left hand or your right hand?

____

I picked a few flowers for my mother.

____

We took a walk along the river.

____

NAME: ______________________________

Directions: Find the words from the word bank among the scrambled letters, and circle them. Then, unscramble the letters below to create the words. Write the words three times each.

Word Bank

left don't few while along

alongdospemskdontskdisodfwevndksleislitskdfos

kleftdksodkfhsdkflwhiledkfosimelsdlfdksofewfkd

1. glano ______________________________
2. felt ______________________________
3. iwlhe ______________________________
4. ewf ______________________________
5. n'dto ______________________________

Play with the Words

NAME: ____________________

Directions: Color in the words. Then, trace around each word six times to create a rainbow of red, orange, yellow, green, blue, and purple.

left

don't

few

while

along

NAME: ______________________________

Directions: Read each sentence, and highlight the word from the word bank. Then, compare each sentence pair, and put a star next to the one that makes sense.

Word Bank

left don't few while along

1a. I had to wait a few minutes for my mom.

1b. There are a few letters in the alphabet.

2a. I saw a huge while at the aquarium.

2b. She listened to music while she was working.

3a. I cut along piece of ribbon for the gift.

3b. Come along with me to the store.

4a. Father left the keys in the car.

4b. I want to left for the movie.

5a. I don't like to clean my room.

5b. She don't like to eat broccoli.

Write the Words

NAME: ______________________________

Directions: Write three sentences about the picture. Use as many words from the word bank as you can in each sentence. Underline the words.

Word Bank

left don't few while along

1. ______________________________
____

2. ______________________________
____

3. ______________________________
____

Challenge: Draw a star next to the sentence that has the most words of the week.

NAME: ______________________________

Directions: Color each word, and circle it in the sentence. Cut out the cards. Then, staple or tape the cards together to make a book.

might

It is very cold and might snow tonight.

close

Can you close the door when you leave?

something

I want something sweet to eat.

seem

Long car rides seem to last forever!

next

Next week is my seventh birthday party.

NAME: ______________________________

Directions: Find and highlight each of the words. (Hint: Each word appears five times.)

Word Bank

might close something seem next

seem	might	seem	might
close	example	closed	got
next	something	close	run
net	begin	next	close
text	close	seem	something
nix	life	see	cloth
next	might	seem	might
might	lose	those	group
next	always	seen	me
next	some	both	something
hard	tight	paper	close
night	seem	together	important
mine	someone	something	often
something	seem		
open	something		
	thing		

NAME: ______________________________

Directions: Work with a friend. Take turns rolling a die 10 times. Match the number you roll to the word, and read the word in a **silly voice**. Place an X in the row next to it. If you roll a six, say all the words.

might	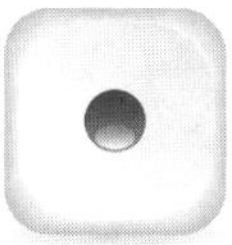	
close	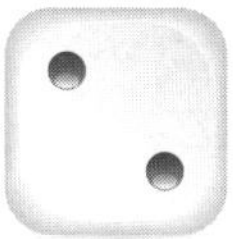	
something		
seem	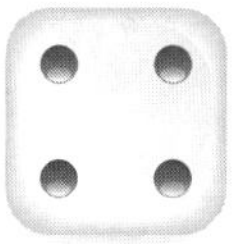	
next		

Challenge: Draw a star next to the sentence that has the most words of the week.

NAME: ____________________________________

Directions: Read each set of words. Circle the word from the word bank. Then, use the word in a sentence.

Word Bank				
might	close	something	seem	next

1. between, seem, clean

____

____

2. toes, slow, close

____

____

3. something, someone, summer

____

____

4. text, next, nest

____

____

5. light, fright, might

____

____

NAME: ______________________________

Directions: Read each phrase in the phrase bank. Write three sentences using at least one phrase from the phrase bank.

Phrase Bank

it might grow   close the door   next to her

something is   it doesn't seem

1. ______________________________

____

2. ______________________________

____

3. ______________________________

____

Challenge: Draw a picture for one of your sentences.

NAME: ______________________________

Directions: Trace each word, then circle that word in the sentence. Cut along the dotted lines to make cards. Punch a hole in each card and place it on a practice ring.

hard

I found a hard rock on the playground.

open

Do not leave the window open!

example

Always set a good example in the hallway.

begin

When does baseball practice begin?

life

We studied the life cycle of a butterfly in science.

NAME: ______________________________

Directions: Read the words in the word bank. Then, find and circle them in the puzzle.

Word Bank

hard open example begin life

L	B	T	D	R	M	E
O	P	E	N	R	X	G
O	G	X	S	A	A	L
F	G	D	M	M	I	H
T	M	P	L	F	D	K
X	L	H	E	N	U	O
E	B	E	G	I	N	D

Play with the Words

NAME: ______________________________

Directions: Write each word. Then, write the word backward.

example: girl lrig

1. hard ______________ ______________
2. open ______________ ______________
3. example ______________ ______________
4. begin ______________ ______________
5. life ______________ ______________

Directions: Write each word in all uppercase letters, then all lowercase letters.

example: GIRL girl

1. example ______________ ______________
2. open ______________ ______________
3. hard ______________ ______________
4. life ______________ ______________
5. begin ______________ ______________

NAME: ______________________________

Directions: Write the correct word from the word bank in the space to complete each sentence. Then, rewrite the sentence on the lines below.

Word Bank

begin open example hard life

1. The jar was ____________ to open.

____

____

2. The movie will ____________ in ten minutes.

____

____

3. I have lived in the country my whole ____________.

____

____

4. The gate to the backyard was left ____________.

____

____

5. I followed the ____________ in the directions.

____

____

Use the Words

Write the Words

NAME: ______________________________

Directions: Write a sentence that includes at least three words from the word bank. Then, draw a picture to go with it.

Word Bank				
hard	open	example	begin	life

____

____

____

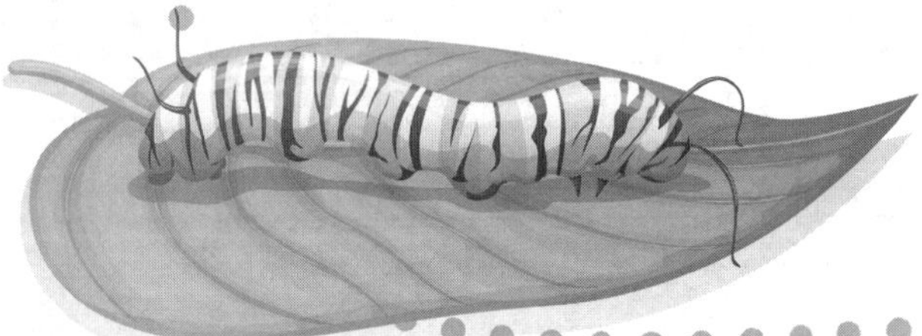

NAME: ______________________________

Directions: Look at each picture, and read the sentence next to it. Circle the word from the word bank in the sentence. Then, write the word on the line.

Word Bank

always   those   both   paper   together

Always eat a healthy breakfast.

____

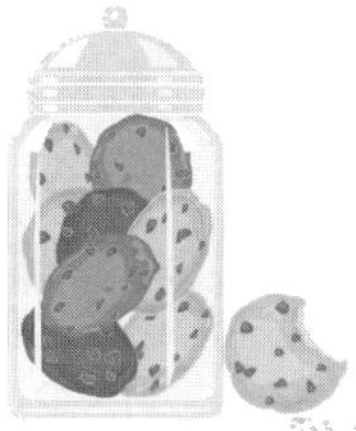

Can I have some of those yummy cookies?

____

I think both of the puppies are cute.

____

The paper is on the desk.

____

He likes to mix paint colors together.

____

Recognize the Words

NAME: ______________________________

Directions: Find the words from the word bank among the scrambled letters, and circle them. Then, unscramble the letters below to create the words. Write the words three times each.

Word Bank

always	those	both	paper	together

f k d l s e a l w a s e d k f o s l d a l w a y s f k d o s p a p e r k d l f b o t h g

f k d o s d o t n s k d o s d l f t o g e t h e r l s d i f l d s i t h o s e l d i f l s o d

1. erapp ______________________________
2. wayals ______________________________
3. hstoe ______________________________
4. obht ______________________________
5. eerhttgo ______________________________

NAME: ______________________________

Directions: Color in the words. Then, trace around each word six times to create a rainbow of red, orange, yellow, green, blue, and purple.

always

those

both

paper

together

Use the Words

NAME: ______________________________

Directions: Read each sentence, and highlight the word from the word bank. Then, compare each sentence pair, and put a star next to the one that makes sense.

Word Bank

always those both paper together

1a. When is the paper at?

1b. Don't forget to write your name on the paper.

2a. We like to play catch together.

2b. Sue likes together leaves and sticks.

3a. The dog and cat are both sleeping.

3b. He wants all or both of the candy.

4a. There are always of making a bed.

4b. You should always make your bed.

5a. I don't want none of those cookies.

5b. Would you like two of those cookies?

NAME: ______________________________

Directions: Write three sentences about the picture. Use as many words from the word bank as you can in each sentence. Underline the words.

Word Bank

always	those	both	paper	together

1. ______________________________

____

2. ______________________________

____

3. ______________________________

____

Challenge: Draw a star next to the sentence that has the most words of the week.

NAME: ______________________________

Directions: Color each word, and circle it in the sentence. Cut out the cards. Then, staple or tape the cards together to make a book.

got

She got a good grade on her test.

group

The group of boys played kickball.

often

It rains often in India.

run

I like to run and play with my dog.

important

It is important to do your homework.

NAME: ____________________

Directions: Find and highlight each of the words. (Hint: Each word appears five times.)

Word Bank				
got	group	often	run	important

important	often	tent	car
got	run	port	feet
not	night	important	until
go	run	important	mile
tot	group	got	run
offer	grass	off	walk
group	soup	ten	white
got	important	got	sea
often	mop	fun	river
group	group	often	took
often	got	run	four
ran	group	run	began
often	important	children	grow
fan	import	side	

NAME: ______________________________

Directions: Work with a friend. Take turns rolling a die 10 times. Match the number you roll to the word, and read the word in a funny voice. Place an X in the row next to it. If you roll a six, mark and say all the words.

often		
run		
important		
group	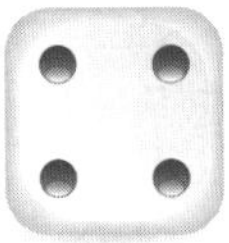	
got		

Challenge: Which word did you roll the most?

____

NAME: ______________________________

Directions: Read each set of words. Circle the word from the word bank. Then, use the word in a sentence.

Word Bank

often group important run got

1. sun, run, ran

____

____

2. group, troop, grip

____

____

3. airport, important, sentence

____

____

4. get, trot, got

____

____

5. soften, often, off

____

____

NAME: ____

Directions: Read each phrase in the phrase bank. Write three sentences using at least one phrase in each from the phrase bank.

Phrase Bank

she often ate | it is important | run for president | he got a | the green group

1. ____
____

2. ____
____

3. ____
____

Challenge: Draw a picture for one of your sentences.

NAME: ______________________________

Directions: Trace each word, then circle that word in the sentence. Cut along the dotted lines to make cards. Punch a hole in each card and place it on a practice ring.

until

We cannot go until the bell rings!

children

The children like to sing and dance.

side

Write your name on the left side of the paper.

feet

How many feet are in a yard?

car

The car is parked under the tree.

Recognize the Words

NAME: ____________________

Directions: Read the words in the word bank. Then, find and circle them in the puzzle.

Word Bank

children side car feet until

Q	R	I	Q	N	I	S	M	F
A	T	I	W	M	F	T	N	E
B	C	M	K	I	T	J	D	R
S	A	E	D	P	Z	I	A	O
U	N	T	I	L	S	C	Y	G
C	H	I	L	D	R	E	N	X
F	E	E	T	H	S	O	P	T
X	N	E	V	Q	N	X	O	U
H	Y	S	T	L	S	C	Y	F

NAME: ____________________

Directions: Write each word. Then, write the word backward.

example: class ssalc

1. children ____________ ____________
2. car ____________ ____________
3. feet ____________ ____________
4. side ____________ ____________
5. until ____________ ____________

Directions: Write each word in uppercase letters, then write the word in lowercase letters.

example: CLASS class

1. side ____________ ____________
2. until ____________ ____________
3. children ____________ ____________
4. car ____________ ____________
5. feet ____________ ____________

NAME: ______________________________

Directions: Write the correct word from the word bank in the space to complete each sentence. Then, rewrite the sentence on the lines below.

Word Bank				
children	side	car	feet	until

1. There are four ____________ in my family.

   ____

   ____

2. My uncle will pick me up in his ____________.

   ____

   ____

3. How many ____________ are in a mile?

   ____

   ____

4. I counted each ____________ of the cube.

   ____

   ____

5. I waited ____________ my mother came home.

   ____

   ____

NAME: ____

Directions: Write a sentence that includes at least three words from the word bank. Then, draw a picture to go with it.

Word Bank

until	car	side	feet	children

____

____

____

NAME: ______________________________

Directions: Look at each picture, and read the sentence next to it. Circle the word from the word bank in the sentence. Then, write the word on the line.

Word Bank

mile night walk white sea

Margaret took her dog for a walk.

____

Do you like to swim in the sea?

____

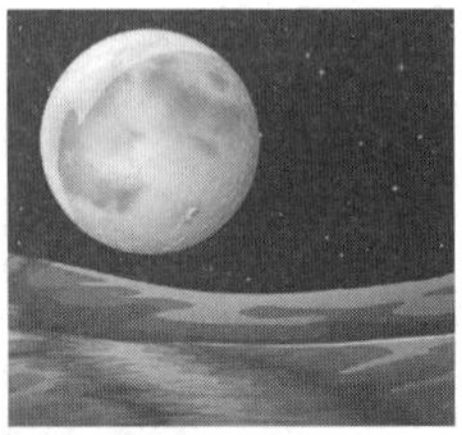

The moon lit up the night sky.

____

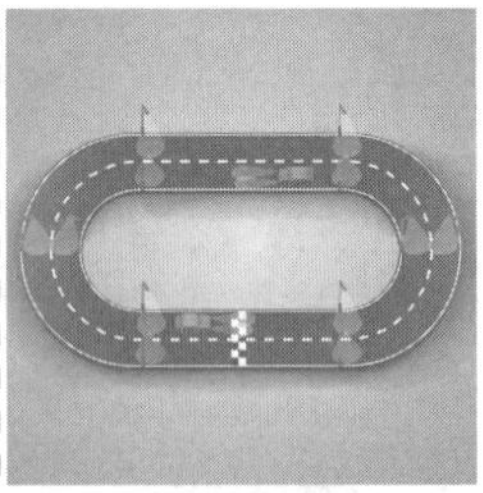

The race was one mile long.

____

The man's teeth are white.

____

NAME: ______________________________

Directions: Find the words from the word bank among the scrambled letters, and circle them. Then, unscramble the letters below to create the words. Write the words three times each.

Word Bank				
walk	mile	night	sea	white

dkfoswhitesldifsldiaomiledkfosldinitelsidlslaisl

walkdflsidlfisdfnightdksdfsldiaseesldifsealdifln

1. elmi ______________________________
2. esa ______________________________
3. htiwe ______________________________
4. ghnti ______________________________
5. lwka ______________________________

NAME: ______________________________

Directions: Color in the words. Then, trace around each word six times to create a rainbow of red, orange, yellow, green, blue, and purple.

white

sea

mile

night

walk

NAME: ____

Directions: Read each sentence, and highlight the word from the word bank. Then, compare each sentence pair, and put a star next to the one that makes sense.

Word Bank

sea walk night mile white

1a. Every night, the sun goes down.

1b. He is the king, and I am the night.

2a. The snow was cold and white.

2b. I want to leave white this minute.

3a. Yesterday, we walk for thirty minutes.

3b. Bill took a walk with his sister, Kate.

4a. I can hear the sea from my bedroom window.

4b. I can sea for miles from the top of the mountain.

5a. The school is one mile from my house.

5b. Grandma's house is thirty mile from where I live.

Write the Words

NAME: ____

Directions: Write three sentences about the picture. Use as many words from the word bank as you can in each sentence. Underline the words.

Word Bank				
night	mile	walk	white	sea

1. ____

____

2. ____

____

3. ____

____

Challenge: Draw a star next to the sentence that has the most high-frequency words.

NAME: ____________________

Directions: Color each word, and circle it in the sentence. Cut out the cards. Then, staple or tape the cards together to make a book.

began

It became cloudy and began to rain.

grow

The tree should grow three feet this year.

took

Isabelle's father took us to the movie.

river

The sailboat floated down the river.

four

Can four people fit in your car?

NAME: ______________________________

Directions: Find and highlight each of the words.
(Hint: Each word appears five times.)

Word Bank

began   river   four   grow   took

river	begun	took	once
never	grow	began	carry
ever	took	river	state
rye	four	began	stop
river	for	river	without
began	our	grow	second
river	from	grass	late
began	four	mow	miss
took	four	row	eat
look	grow	grow	enough
tool	four	four	idea
book	began	took	face
took	be	grow	watch
	begin		

NAME: ____

Directions: Work with a friend. Take turns rolling a die 10 times. Match the number you roll to the word, and read the word in a funny voice. Place an X in the row next to it. If you roll a six, mark and say all the words.

four	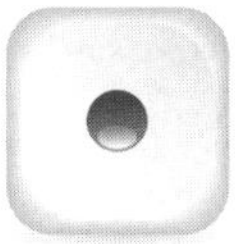	
began		
river		
took		
grow		

Challenge: Which word did you roll the most?

____

NAME: ______________________________

Directions: Read each set of words. Circle the word from the word bank. Then, use the word in a sentence.

Word Bank				
grow	took	four	began	river

1. four, soar, for

____

____

2. throw, row, grow

____

____

3. shiver, river, under

____

____

4. before, begin, began

____

____

5. took, take, look

____

____

NAME: ______________________________

Directions: Read each phrase in the phrase bank. Write three sentences using at least one phrase from the phrase bank.

Phrase Bank

who took | can they grow | four groups of | clean the river | began to cry

1. ______________________________

____

2. ______________________________

____

3. ______________________________

____

Challenge: Draw a picture for one of your sentences.

Introduce the Words

NAME: ______________________________

Directions: Color each word, then circle that word in the sentence. Cut along the dotted lines to make word cards. Punch a hole in each card and place it on a practice ring.

carry

I helped my aunt carry in the groceries.

state

Which state do you want to visit?

once

I call my grandpa once a week.

book

This book is amazing!

hear

I can hear the wind blow during the storm.

NAME: ____

Directions: Read the words in the word bank. Then, find and circle them in the puzzle.

Word Bank

book hear once carry state

A	B	O	O	K	F	T	M	E
W	U	S	R	B	F	A	R	I
X	U	S	R	C	F	A	F	C
S	Y	L	O	R	E	M	Y	M
N	T	O	D	H	U	A	R	Z
O	K	A	O	N	C	E	R	F
D	Z	Y	T	H	L	Q	A	Q
Q	N	F	N	E	Z	O	C	H

NAME: ______________________________

Play with the Words

Directions: Write each word. Then, write the word backward.

example: write etirw

1. hear ____________ ____________
2. book ____________ ____________
3. state ____________ ____________
4. once ____________ ____________
5. carry ____________ ____________

Directions: Write each word in uppercase letters, then lowercase letters.

example: WRITE write

1. once ____________ ____________
2. hear ____________ ____________
3. book ____________ ____________
4. state ____________ ____________
5. carry ____________ ____________

Use the Words

NAME: ______________________________

Directions: Write the correct word from the word bank in the space to complete each sentence. Then, rewrite the sentence on the lines below.

Word Bank

once carry state hear book

1. My friend is moving to another ______________.

____

____

2. Do you ______________ that ringing noise?

____

____

3. I can play outside ______________ I finish my dinner.

____

____

4. Can you help me ______________ this heavy box?

____

____

5. The ______________ has sixteen chapters.

____

____

NAME: ____________________

Directions: Write a sentence that includes at least three words from the word bank. Then, draw a picture to go with it.

Word Bank				
state	hear	once	carry	book

____

____

____

NAME: ______________________________

Directions: Look at each picture, and read the sentence next to it. Circle the word from the word bank in the sentence. Then, write the word on the line.

Word Bank

miss	late	second	without	stop

You must stop at the stop sign.

____

I was second in line in the cafeteria.

____

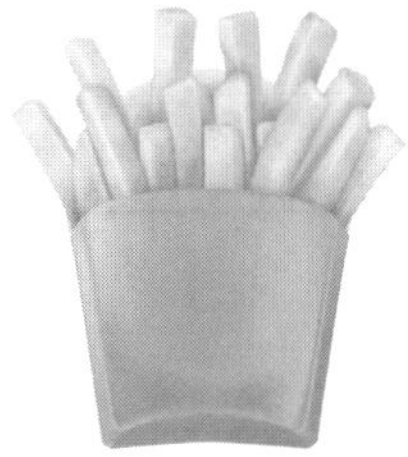

Dan likes french fries without ketchup.

____

Susan woke up early so she wouldn't be late.

____

I didn't want to miss the bus.

____

NAME: ______________________________

Directions: Find the words from the word bank among the scrambled letters, and circle them. Then, unscramble the letters below to create the words. Write the words three times each.

Word Bank

without	stop	miss	second	late

f k d l s t o p s l d f i d l s i d f k d w i h t s l d f k d w i t h o u t s l d f i l s k t

f k d s l a t e s k d f o s d l s e c o n d k s d o f s p a s d f m i s s k d f o s d

1. ssmi ______________________________
2. otutihw ______________________________
3. ospt ______________________________
4. alte ______________________________
5. nocsed ______________________________

NAME: ______________________________

Directions: Color in the words. Then, trace around each word six times to create a rainbow of red, orange, yellow, green, blue, and purple.

miss

late

second

without

stop

NAME: ______________________________

Use the Words

Directions: Read each sentence, and highlight the word from the word bank. Then, compare each sentence pair, and put a star next to the one that makes sense.

Word Bank

second without late miss stop

1a. I went to the bank to without some money.

1b. Do not leave without saying goodbye.

2a. We learn addition facts in second grade.

2b. There are sixty second in one minute.

3a. Yesterday morning, I miss my bus.

3b. Charlie didn't want to miss the movie.

4a. We hiked to the stop of the mountain.

4b. She wanted me to stop playing the video game.

5a. Hurry up, or we'll be late for school!

5b. Don't forget to close the late when you leave.

NAME: ______________________________

Directions: Write three sentences about the picture. Use as many words from the word bank as you can in each sentence. Underline the words.

Word Bank				
stop	without	second	late	miss

1. ______________________________
____

2. ______________________________
____

3. ______________________________
____

Challenge: Draw a star next to the sentence that has the most high-frequency words.

NAME: ______________________________

Directions: Color each word, and circle it in the sentence. Cut out the cards. Then, staple or tape the cards together to make a book.

watch

My family likes to watch television shows.

face

When I was eating ice cream, I got some on my face.

eat

Dad told us we would eat dinner early tonight.

enough

There was enough pizza for everyone.

idea

Do you have any idea what to get Mom for her birthday?

NAME: ______________________________

Directions: Find and highlight each of the words. (Hint: Each word appears five times.)

Word Bank

watch face eat enough idea

eat
ear
at
enough
bought
face
cough
rough
enough
idea
I'd
deal
indent
idea
face
idea
fast

ace
facing
face
idea
face
watch
eat
watching
face
match
eat
much
ate
enough
watch
eat
watch

idea
eat
watch
add
between
every
enough
food
near
start
city
earth
eye
watch
enough
light
got

run
group
important
often
might
close
something
seem
next

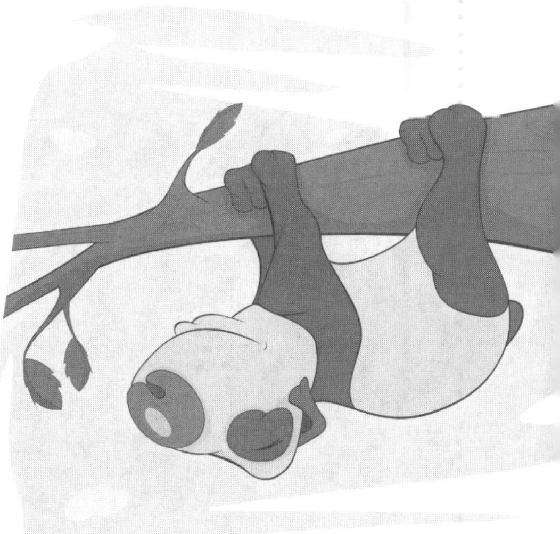

NAME: ______________________________

Directions: Work with a friend. Take turns rolling a die 20 times. Match the number you roll to the word, and read the word in a *robot voice*. Place a tally mark in the row next to the word. If you roll a six, say all the words in the robot voice.

enough	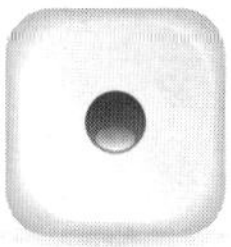	
eat	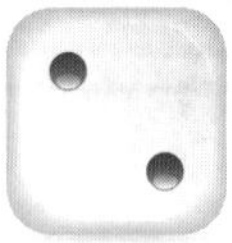	
watch		
idea	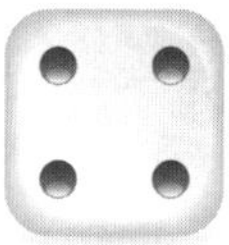	
face		

Challenge: Which word did you roll the most?

____

NAME: ______________________________

Directions: Read each set of words. Circle the word from the word bank. Then, use the word in a sentence.

Word Bank				
watch	face	eat	enough	idea

1. walk, watch, white

____

____

2. through, enough, high

____

____

3. fact, fake, face

____

____

4. eat, treat, feet

____

____

5. eye, light, idea

____

____

Write the Words

NAME: ______________________________

Directions: Read each phrase in the phrase bank. Write three sentences using at least one phrase in each from the phrase bank.

Phrase Bank

enough is enough   can we eat   the brightest idea

the digital watch   sketch his face

1. ______________________________

____

2. ______________________________

____

3. ______________________________

____

Challenge: Draw a picture for one of your sentences.

NAME: ______________________________

Directions: Trace each word, then circle that word in the sentence. Cut along the dotted lines to make cards. Punch a hole in each card and place it on a practice ring.

far

How far can you throw the baseball?

cold

It is very windy and cold today!

real

Is that a real snake?

almost

I am almost finished with the book.

let

My sister let me borrow her new skateboard.

Recognize the Words

NAME: ______________________________

Directions: Read the words in the word bank. Then, find and circle them in the puzzle.

Word Bank

real far cold let almost

C	J	A	M	Z	R	G	X	J
Z	O	M	L	R	A	C	F	C
J	S	L	L	M	F	K	O	W
U	A	C	D	N	O	Q	N	R
P	A	O	R	A	A	S	J	I
B	Y	E	U	V	N	R	T	V
Z	A	A	L	V	H	I	Z	H
L	G	N	P	E	X	Y	Y	W
U	Q	I	Q	D	T	C	R	Y

NAME: ____________________

Directions: Write each word. Then, write the word backward.

example: kitten nettik

1. far ____________ ____________
2. cold ____________ ____________
3. real ____________ ____________
4. let ____________ ____________
5. almost ____________ ____________

Directions: Write each word in uppercase letters, then write the word in lowercase letters.

example: KITTEN kitten

1. cold ____________ ____________
2. far ____________ ____________
3. almost ____________ ____________
4. let ____________ ____________
5. real ____________ ____________

Use the Words

NAME: ______________________________

Directions: Write the correct word from the word bank in the space to complete each sentence. Then, rewrite the sentence on the lines below.

Word Bank

far   cold   real   almost   let

1. This winter will be very ____________.

____

____

2. How ____________ can I run in ten minutes?

____

____

3. John asked, "Did you ____________ the dog out?"

____

____

4. Dad wasn't paying attention and ____________ missed the turn.

____

____

5. Todd wants a ____________ goldfish for his birthday.

____

____

NAME: ______________________________

Write the Words

Directions: Write a sentence that includes at least three words from the word bank. Then, draw a picture to go with it.

Word Bank				
almost	far	cold	let	real

____

____

____

NAME: ____________________

Directions: Look at each picture, and read the sentence next to it. Circle the word from the word bank in the sentence. Then, write the word on the line.

Word Bank

cut   mountain   sometimes   above   girl

The girl is smiling because she's happy.

____

The plane is above the clouds.

____

Sometimes, I like to stay up late and read.

____

The tall mountain is very steep.

____

My mom will cut the birthday cake.

____

NAME: ______________________________

Directions: Find the words from the word bank among the scrambled letters, and circle them. Then, unscramble the letters below to create the words. Write the words three times each.

Word Bank

girl sometimes above cut mountain

d k f s o m e f k d o s l f i s o m e t i m e s l d i f l s d f i f d t y c u t m s i d

s k d o f a b o v e f h g f m o u n t a i n d k f o s l e g i r l b n d k s o f d l o

1. ntounaim ______________________________
2. vboea ______________________________
3. eetosmmis ______________________________
4. rlgi ______________________________
5. utc ______________________________

NAME: ______________________________

Directions: Color in the words. Then, trace around each word six times to create a rainbow of red, orange, yellow, green, blue, and purple.

cut

girl

sometimes

above

mountain

NAME: ______________________________

Directions: Read each sentence, and highlight the word from the word bank. Then, compare each sentence pair, and put a star next to the one that makes sense.

Word Bank

girl sometimes cut mountain above

1a. It took all day to hike up the mountain path.

1b. We went up the mountain to swim in the ocean.

2a. Did you cut the knife with the cake?

2b. The teacher showed us how to cut the paper.

3a. Sometimes, my brother and I argue.

3b. Seven plus two is sometimes nine.

4a. The girl bounced the big red ball nine times.

4b. The girl added one and five to get four.

5a. The school of fish swam above the water.

5b. The tall man can see above the crowd.

NAME: ______________________________

Write the Words

Directions: Write three sentences about the picture. Use as many words from the word bank as you can in each sentence. Underline the words.

Word Bank				
girl	mountain	sometimes	cut	above

1. ______________________________
____

2. ______________________________
____

3. ______________________________
____

Challenge: Draw a star next to the sentence that has the most high-frequency words.

NAME: ______________________________

Directions: Write each word from the word bank one time. Next, color the words at the bottom of the page. Finally, cut along the dotted lines to create flash cards. Keep the cards in a folder to practice each day.

Word Bank

young	talk	soon	list	song

______________________ ______________________

______________________ ______________________

____

young	
soon	talk
song	list

NAME: ______________________________

Directions: Draw a square around the word **young**. Draw a circle around the word **talk.** Draw a triangle around the word **soon.** Draw a rectangle around the word **list.** Underline the word **song.**

list soon talk young

young song soon talk

list song talk young

soon song list

Challenge: Write each word twice in your own fun font.

1. ______________________________

2. ______________________________

3. ______________________________

4. ______________________________

5. ______________________________

NAME: ______________________________

Directions: Follow the directions below to play a memory game.

1. Cut apart the word cards below.
2. Place the cards facedown so you can't see the words.
3. Turn over one card, say the word, and spell it.
4. Turn over another card.
5. If the words are the same, keep the cards facing up.
6. If the words are different, turn the cards over and try again.
7. Continue playing until all the cards are facing up.

young	talk	
young	soon	
talk	soon	list
song	list	song

NAME: ______________________________

Directions: Read the paragraph. Fill in each blank space with the best word from the word bank. Some words may be used more than once.

Word Bank				
young	talk	soon	list	song

Hayley's family will go shopping __________. Her mom is making a __________ of things to buy. On the drive to the store, Hayley's family will __________ and sing a __________. Her brother is too __________ to __________ and sing the __________. She hopes he will be able to __________ and sing __________.

Challenge: Which word did you use the most?

____

NAME: ______________________________

Directions: Write three sentences. In each sentence, use one word from the word bank and one phrase from the phrase bank.

Word Bank

young talk soon list song

Phrase Bank

in line listen to the along the way
stay awhile in the beginning

1. ______________________________

____

____

2. ______________________________

____

____

3. ______________________________

____

____

____

Introduce the Words

NAME: ____

Directions: Read each sentence. Highlight the word from the word bank. Write the word on the line. Cut along the dotted lines to make cards. Staple or tape the cards together to make a book.

Word Bank				
being	leave	family	it's	afternoon

The family is going on a picnic.

____

I go to soccer practice in the afternoon.

____

We will leave at three o'clock.

____

I like being part of the team.

____

When it's raining, we can't play outside.

____

NAME: ______________________

Directions: Write the words from the word bank in alphabetical order. Then, write the words in reverse alphabetical order.

Word Bank

being leave family it's afternoon

Alphabetical Order

1. ______________________
2. ______________________
3. ______________________
4. ______________________
5. ______________________

Reverse Alphabetical Order

1. ______________________
2. ______________________
3. ______________________
4. ______________________
5. ______________________

a b c d e f g h i j k l m n o p q r s t u v w x y z

NAME: ______________________________

Directions: Cut out the letter tiles. Use them to make the words in the word bank. Glue the words on a separate sheet of paper.

Word Bank

being leave family it's afternoon

a	a	a	b	e
e	e	e	f	f
g	i	i	i	l
l	m	n	n	n
o	o	s	t	t
v	’	r	y	

NAME: ______________________________

Directions: Read the beginning of each sentence. Circle the word from the word bank. Then, use your imagination to write a creative ending.

Word Bank				
being	leave	family	it's	afternoon

1. Don't leave the door open, or ______________________________
____
2. It's very hard to ______________________________
____
3. The best thing about being a second grader is ______
____
4. My family likes to ______________________________
____
5. This afternoon I want to ______________________________
____

NAME: ______________________________

Write the Words

Directions: Use the cursive letters below to write each word three times. Make sure to connect the letters in each word.

a b c d e f g h i j k l m n
o p q r s t u v w x y z

example: name *name*

being ______________________________

____

leave ______________________________

____

family ______________________________

____

it's ______________________________

____

____

afternoon ______________________________

____

____

NAME: ______________________________

Directions: Look at the picture in each box. Write the word from the word bank that goes with the picture. Cut out the cards. Punch a hole in each card and place it on your practice ring.

Word Bank

color music body stand sun

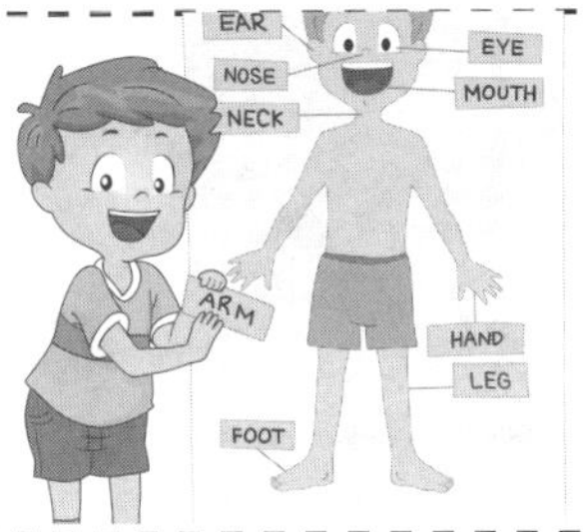

1. ______________________

2. ______________________

3. ______________________

4. ______________________

5. ______________________

Recognize the Words

NAME: ______________________________

Directions: Write each word three times. First, write the word in pencil. Next, write the word in crayon. Then, write the word in marker.

Word Bank

body music color stand sun

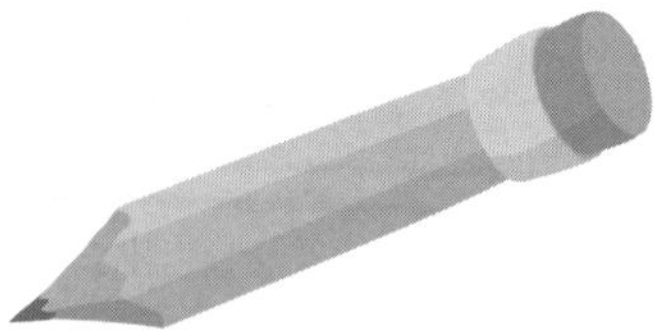	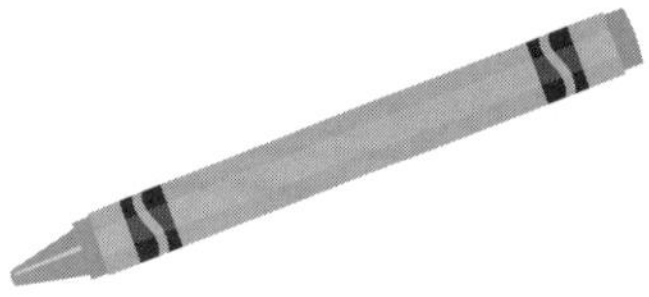	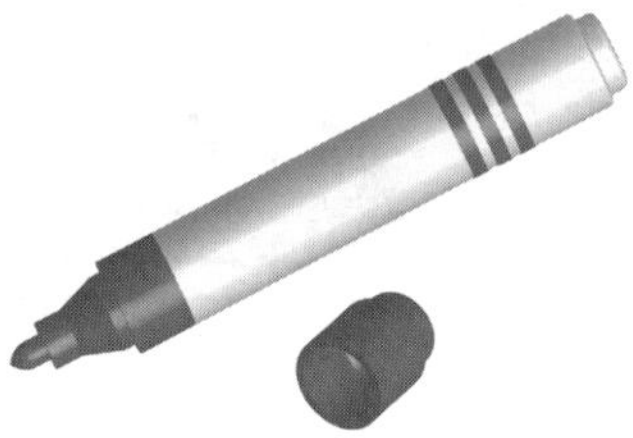

NAME: ______________________________

Directions: Find each letter on the telephone. For each letter, write the number that matches it. Add the numbers together. How much is each word?

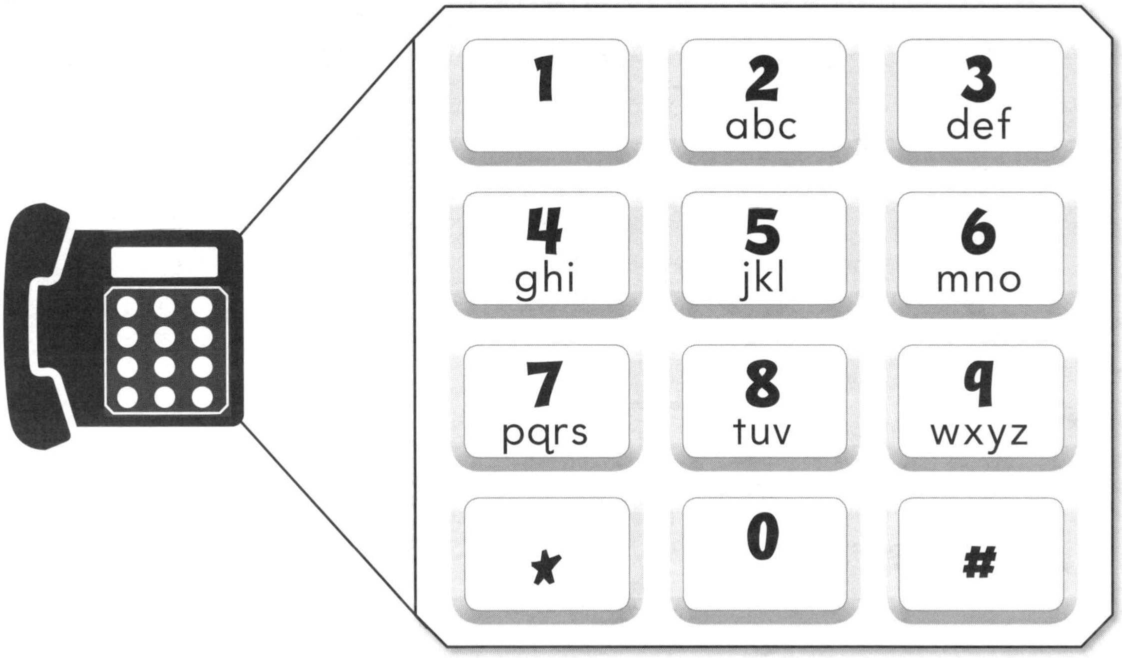

example: worm 9 + 6 + 7 + 6 = 28

1. body ______________________________
2. sun ______________________________
3. music ______________________________
4. color ______________________________
5. stand ______________________________

Challenge: Which word has the highest value?

____

Use the Words

NAME: ______________________________

Directions: Use the words and the code below to color in the image.

brown:	**red:**	**blue:**	**green**	**yellow**
music	sun	color	stand	body

NAME: ____________________________

Directions: Pretend you are in the scene below and write a story about what is happening. Use as many words from the word bank as you can.

Word Bank				
music	sun	color	stand	body

____

____

____

____

____

____

Challenge: Underline the words you used from the word bank, and read your story to a friend.

NAME: ____________________

Directions: Write each word from the word bank one time. Next, color the words at the bottom of the page. Finally, cut along the dotted lines to create flash cards. Keep the cards in a folder to practice each day.

Word Bank				
questions	fish	area	mark	dog

____________________ ____________________

____________________ ____________________

____

questions

fish

area

mark

dog

NAME: ____________________

Directions: Draw a square around the word **fish.** Draw a circle around the word **dog.** Draw a triangle around the word **mark**. Draw a rectangle around the word **questions**. Underline the word **area**.

area

questions

mark

fish

fish

dog

area

area

dog

questions

mark

fish

mark

dog

questions

Challenge: Write each word twice in your own fun font.

1. ____________________

2. ____________________

3. ____________________

4. ____________________

5. ____________________

Play with the Words

NAME: ______________________________

Directions: Follow the directions below to play a memory game.

1. Cut apart the word cards below.
2. Place the cards facedown so you can't see the words.
3. Turn over one card, say the word, and spell it.
4. Turn over another card.
5. If the words are the same, keep the cards facing up.
6. If the words are different, turn the cards over and try again.
7. Continue playing until all the cards are facing up.

fish	**area**	
fish	**area**	
questions	**mark**	**mark**
questions	**mark**	**dog**

NAME: ______________________________

Directions: Read the paragraph. Fill in each blank space with the best word from the word bank. Some words may be used more than once.

Word Bank				
fish	area	questions	mark	dog

I can't have a pet ______________ because dogs make me sneeze. Dad took me to the pet store to buy a ______________ for a pet. The ______________ tank ______________ was full of colorful ______________. My dad had a lot of ______________ about taking care of ______________. I picked a pretty yellow ______________ with a black ______________ on its tail.

Challenge: Which word did you use the most?

____

NAME: ______________________________

Directions: Write three sentences. In each sentence, use one word from the word bank and one phrase from the phrase bank.

Word Bank

fish area questions mark dog

Phrase Bank

plant the trees you might be right next time
too soon in my head

1. ______________________________

____

2. ______________________________

____

3. ______________________________

____

NAME: ____________________

Directions: Read each sentence. Highlight the word from the word bank. Write the word on the line. Cut along the dotted lines to make cards. Staple or tape the cards together to make a book.

Word Bank

problem	complete	birds	horse	room

The birds flew above the trees.

____

The brown horse ate the hay.

____

I share a room with my twin sister.

____

Tom had a problem tying his shoes.

____

The picture will be complete after I color it.

____

Recognize the Words

NAME: ____________________

Directions: Write the words from the word bank in alphabetical order. Then, write the words in reverse alphabetical order.

Word Bank				
problem	complete	birds	horse	room

Alphabetical Order

1. ____________________
2. ____________________
3. ____________________
4. ____________________
5. ____________________

Reverse Alphabetical Order

1. ____________________
2. ____________________
3. ____________________
4. ____________________
5. ____________________

a b c d e f g h i j k l m n o p q r s t u v w x y z

NAME: ____

Play with the Words

Directions: Cut out the letter tiles. Use them to make the words in the word bank. Glue the words on a separate sheet of paper.

Word Bank

problem complete birds horse room

b	b	c	d	e
e	e	e	h	i
l	l	m	m	m
o	o	o	o	o
p	p	r	r	r
r	s	s	t	

NAME: ____

Directions: Read the beginning of each sentence. Circle the word from the word bank. Then, use your imagination to write a creative ending.

Word Bank

problem complete birds horse room

1. The birds flew below the ______________________

____

2. The problem with worms is ____________________

____

3. I wanted to complete _________________________

____

4. In my room, I have __________________________

____

5. The tiny horse _____________________________

____

NAME: ______________________________

Directions: Use the cursive letters below to write each word three times. Make sure to connect the letters in each word.

a b c d e f g h i j k l m n
o p q r s t u v w x y z

example: zip *zip*

problem ______________________________

____

complete ______________________________

____

horse ______________________________

____

room ______________________________

____

____

bird ______________________________

____

____

NAME: ______________________

Directions: Trace each word, then circle that word in the sentence. Cut along the dotted lines to make cards. Punch a hole in each card and place it on a practice ring.

knew

Sarah knew how to ride a bike.

ever

This is the best cake I've ever had!

since

They have known each other since kindergarten.

piece

Can I have another piece of pie?

told

Mom told me I couldn't go outside.

NAME: ______________________________

Directions: Write each word three times. First, write the word in pencil. Next, write the word in crayon. Then, write the word in marker.

Word Bank

knew since ever piece told

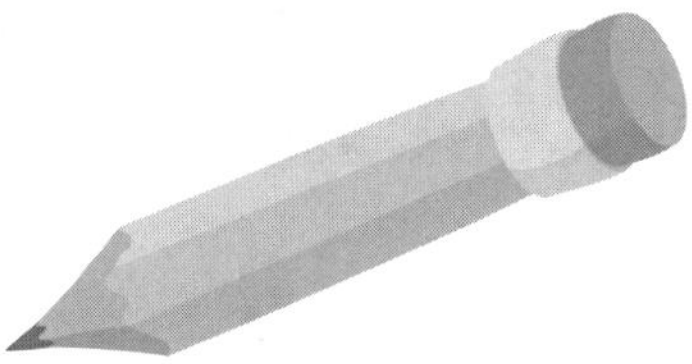	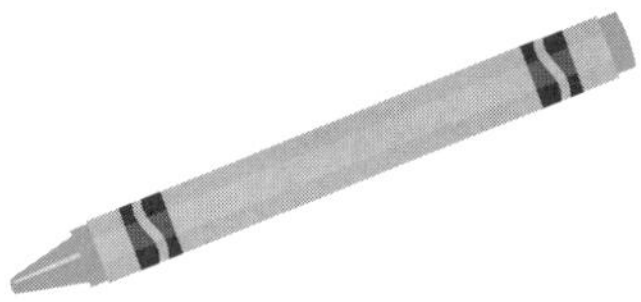	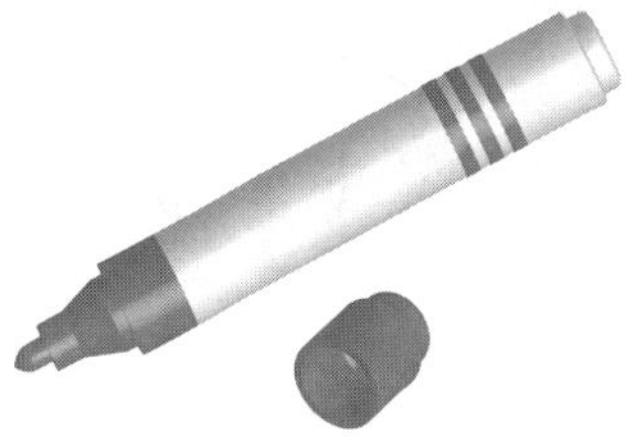

NAME: ______________________________

Directions: Find each letter on the telephone. For each letter, write the number that matches it. Add the numbers together. How much is each word?

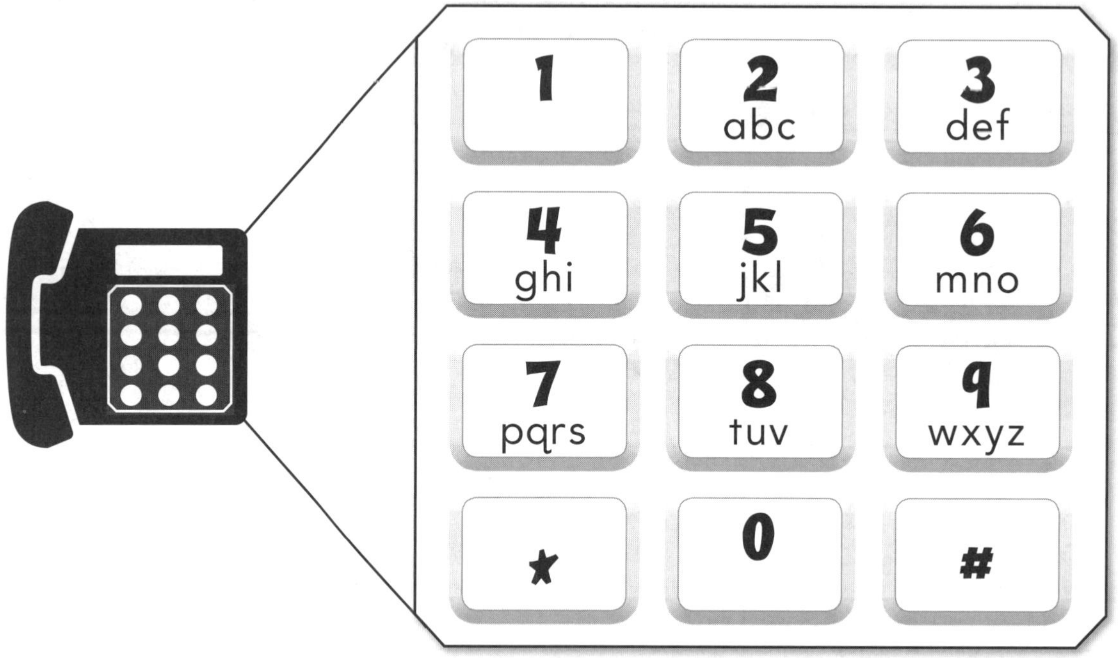

example: book <u>2 + 6 + 6 + 5 = 19</u>

1. knew ______________________________
2. since ______________________________
3. ever ______________________________
4. piece ______________________________
5. told ______________________________

Challenge: Which word has the highest value?

____

NAME: ____

Directions: Use the words and the code below to color in the image.

brown:	**red:**	**blue:**	**green**	**grey**
since	ever	told	piece	knew

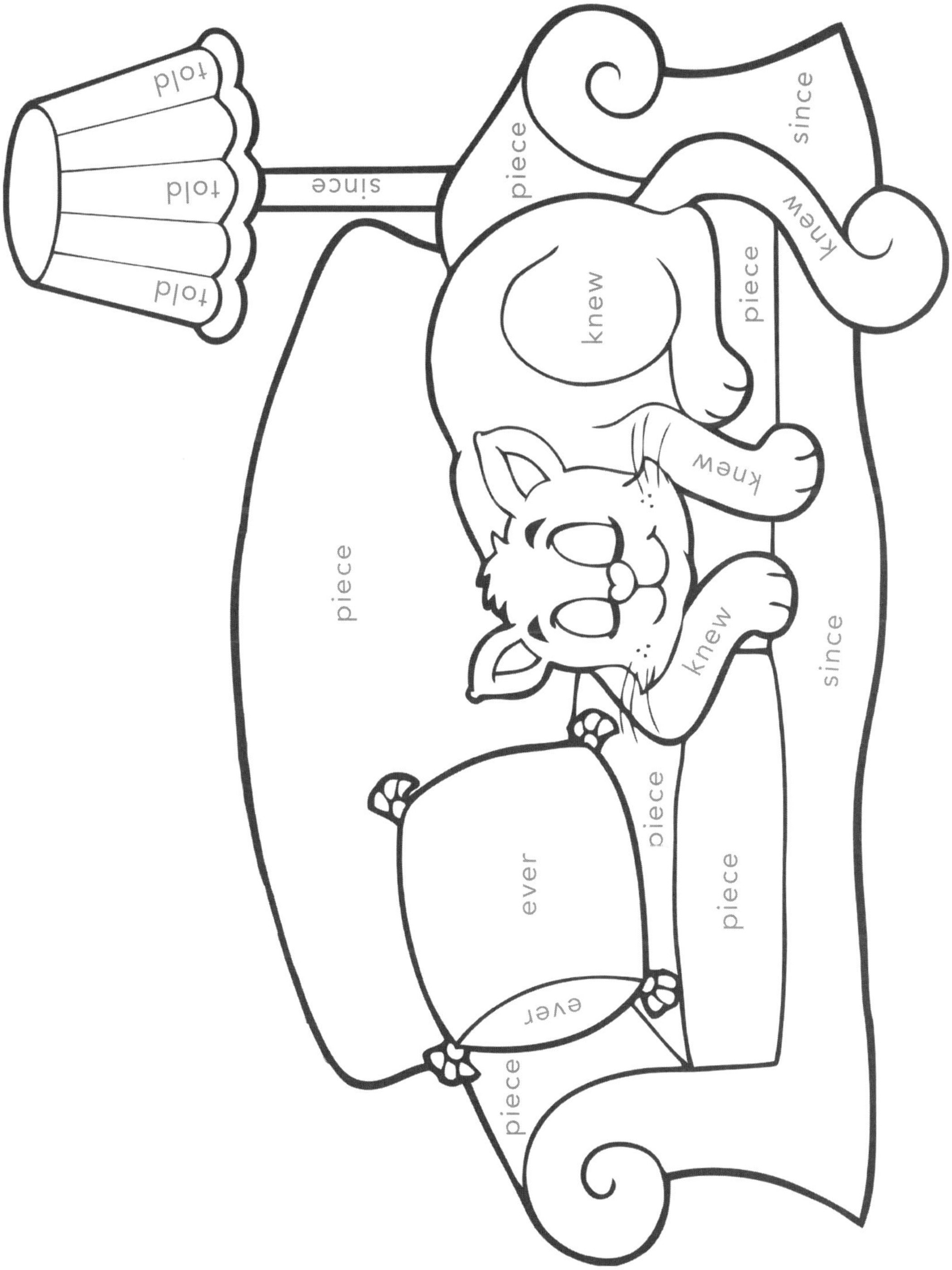

NAME: ____________________

Directions: Pretend you are in the scene below and write a story about what is happening. Use as many words from the word bank as you can.

Word Bank				
knew	since	ever	piece	told

____

____

____

____

____

____

Challenge: Underline the words you used from the word bank, and read your story to a friend.

NAME: ______________________________

Directions: Write each word from the word bank one time. Next, color the words at the bottom of the page. Finally, cut along the dotted lines to create flash cards. Keep the cards in a folder to practice each day.

Word Bank				
usually	didn't	friends	easy	heard

______________________ ______________________

______________________ ______________________

____

usually

didn't friends

easy heard

NAME: ____________________

Directions: Draw a square around the word **friends.** Draw a circle around the word **didn't.** Draw a triangle around the word **usually**. Draw a rectangle around the word **heard.** Underline the word **easy.**

easy friends didn't
usually
didn't
heard usually friends
heard
easy friends didn't
usually heard easy

Challenge: Write each word twice in your own fun font.

1. ______________________________

2. ______________________________

3. ______________________________

4. ______________________________

5. ______________________________

NAME: ______________________________

Directions: Follow the directions below to play a memory game.

1. Cut apart the word cards below.
2. Place the cards facedown so you can't see the words.
3. Turn over one card, say the word, and spell it.
4. Turn over another card.
5. If the words are the same, keep the cards facing up.
6. If the words are different, turn the cards over and try again.
7. Continue playing until all the cards are facing up.

friends	easy	
friends	easy	
usually	didn't	heard
usually	heard	didn't

NAME: ______________________________

Directions: Read the paragraph. Fill in each blank space with the best word from the word bank. Some words may be used more than once.

Word Bank

heard   easy   usually   didn't   friends

My ______________, Jake and Amy, ______________ play with me after school. We like to play outside. It's fun and ______________ to think of things to do. On the radio, we ______________ it was going to rain all day. We ______________ let the rain spoil our fun. Good ______________ can have fun playing inside, too.

Challenge: Which word did you use the most?

____

NAME: ______________________________

Directions: Write three sentences. In each sentence, use one word from the word bank and one phrase from the phrase bank.

Word Bank

friends easy heard didn't usually

Phrase Bank

help me out near the car answer the phone my last name try your best

1. ______________________________

____

2. ______________________________

____

3. ______________________________

____

NAME: ______________________________

Directions: Read each sentence. Highlight the word from the word bank. Write the word on the line. Cut along the dotted lines to make cards. Staple or tape the cards together to make a book.

Word Bank

sure	become	door	red	order

"Can I take your order?" asked the waiter.

____

The boy's bike is bright red.

____

Ryan and I have become good friends.

____

I wasn't sure where I left my hat.

____

Please close the door when you leave.

____

NAME: ______________________________

Directions: Write the words from the word bank in alphabetical order. Then, write the words in reverse alphabetical order.

Word Bank

sure	become	door	red	order

Alphabetical Order

1. ______________________________
2. ______________________________
3. ______________________________
4. ______________________________
5. ______________________________

Reverse Alphabetical Order

1. ______________________________
2. ______________________________
3. ______________________________
4. ______________________________
5. ______________________________

a b c d e f g h i j k l m n o p q r s t u v w x y z

NAME: ____________________

Directions: Cut out the letter tiles. Use them to make the words in the word bank. Glue the words on a separate sheet of paper.

Word Bank

red order door become sure

b	c	d	d	d
e	e	e	e	e
m	o	o	o	o
r	r	r	r	r
s	u			

NAME: ____

Directions: Read the beginning of each sentence. Circle the word from the word bank. Then, use your imagination to write a creative ending.

Word Bank				
red	order	door	sure	become

1. I wish I could become a ______________________

____

2. Can I order a ______________________________

____

3. She knocked on the door and __________________

____

4. The huge red ________________________________

____

5. Matthew was sure he _________________________

____

NAME: ________________________________

Directions: Use the cursive letters below to write each word three times. Make sure to connect the letters in each word.

a b c d e f g h i j k l m n
o p q r s t u v w x y z

example: each *each*

red ________________________________

____

order ________________________________

____

door ________________________________

____

sure ________________________________

____

____

become ________________________________

____

____

NAME: ____

Directions: Look at the picture in each box. Write the word from the word bank that goes with the picture. Cut out the cards. Punch a hole in each card and place it on your practice ring.

Word Bank

top   ship   across   today   during

1. ______________________

2. ______________________

3. ______________________

4. ______________________

5. ______________________

Recognize the Words

NAME: ______________________________

Directions: Write each word three times. First, write the word in pencil. Next, write the word in crayon. Then, write the word in marker.

Word Bank

top   ship   across   today   during

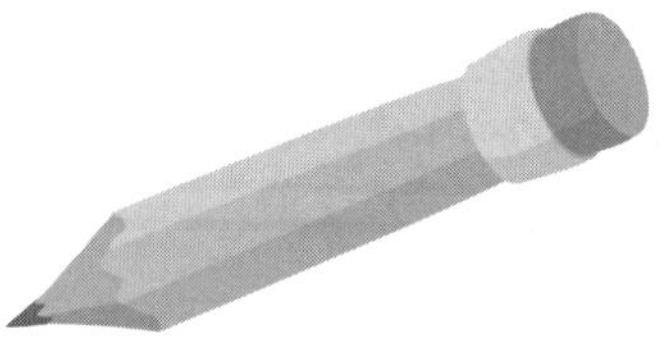	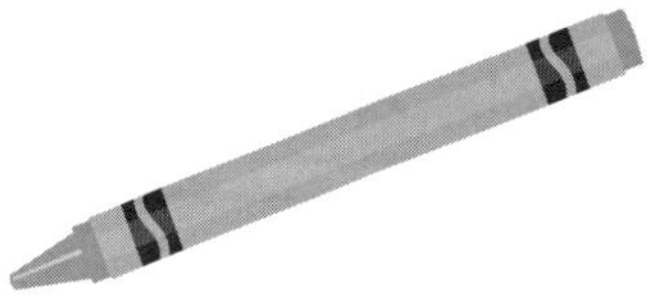	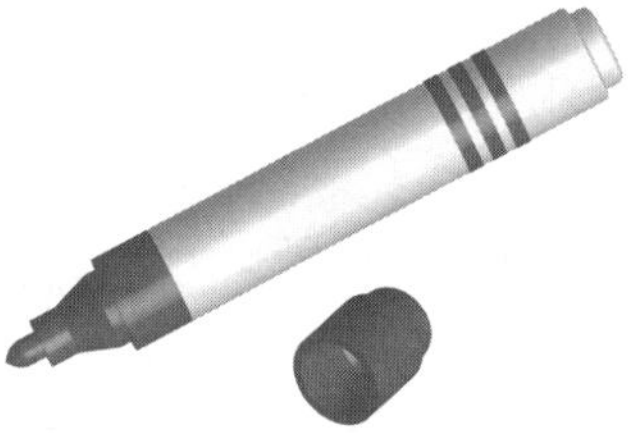

NAME: ______________________________

Directions: Find each letter on the telephone. For each letter, write the number that matches it. Add the numbers together. How much is each word?

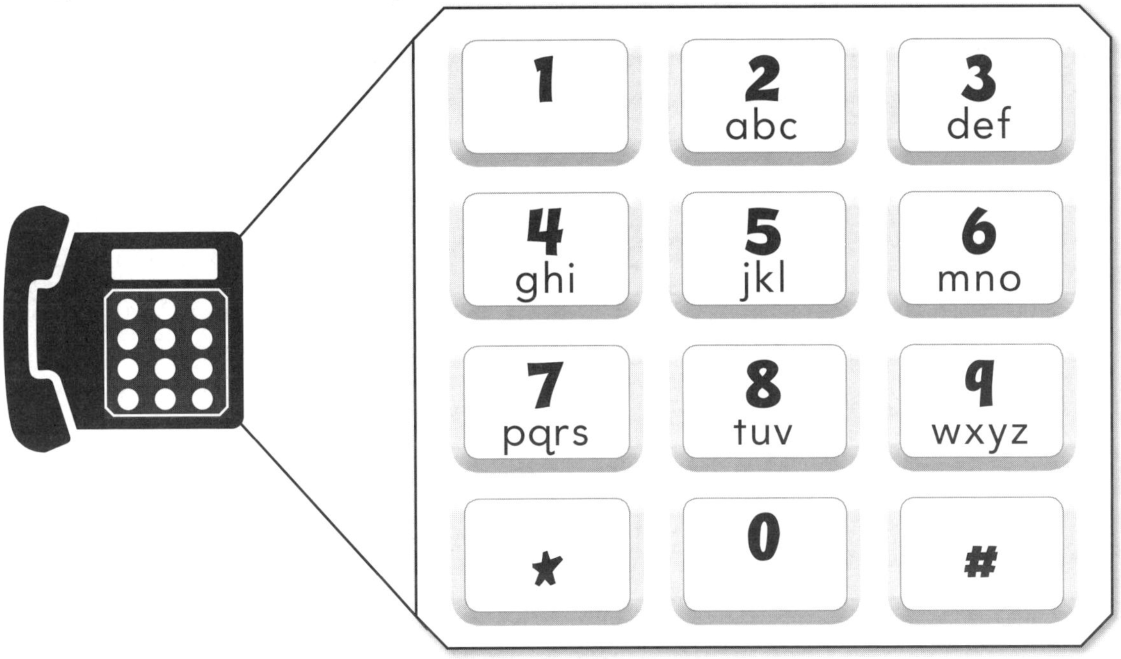

example: sing 7 + 4 + 6 + 4 = 21

1. during ______________________________

2. across ______________________________

3. ship ______________________________

4. top ______________________________

5. today ______________________________

Challenge: Which word has the highest value?

____

Use the Words

NAME: ____________________

Directions: Use the words and the code below to color in the image.

brown:	**red:**	**blue:**	**green:**	**light blue:**
across	top	ship	during	today

NAME: ______________________________

Directions: Pretend you are in the scene below and write a story about what is happening. Use as many words from the word bank as you can.

Word Bank				
top	ship	across	today	during

____

____

____

____

____

____

Challenge: Underline the words you used from the word bank, and read your story to a friend.

Introduce the Words

NAME: ____________________

Directions: Write each word from the word bank one time. Next, color the words at the bottom of the page. Finally, cut along the dotted lines to create flash cards. Keep the cards in a folder to practice each day.

Word Bank

short better best however low

____________________ ____________________

____________________ ____________________

____

short

better

best

however

low

NAME: ______________________________

Directions: Draw a square around the word **short**. Draw a circle around the word **best**. Draw a triangle around the word **low**. Draw a rectangle around the word **however**. Underline the word **better**.

better best however low

low best short however

short however better low

best short better

Recognize the Words

Challenge: Write each word twice in your own fun font.

1. ______________________________

2. ______________________________

3. ______________________________

4. ______________________________

5. ______________________________

NAME: ______________________________

Directions: Follow the directions below to play a memory game.

1. Cut apart the word cards below.
2. Place the cards facedown so you can't see the words.
3. Turn over one card, say the word, and spell it.
4. Turn over another card.
5. If the words are the same, keep the cards facing up.
6. If the words are different, turn the cards over and try again.
7. Continue playing until all the cards are facing up.

short	better	
short	better	
however	low	best
however	best	low

NAME: ____________________________________

Directions: Read the paragraph. Fill in each blank space with the best word from the word bank. Some words may be used more than once.

Word Bank

short	better	best	however	low

At the library, Jaden and Peter looked for ________________ books. The librarian told them they could talk; ________________, they had to keep their voices ________________. Jaden read her book and whispered, "This is the ________________ book ever!" In a ________________ voice, Peter said his book was even ________________.

Challenge: Which word did you use the most?

____

NAME: ______________________________

Directions: Write three sentences. In each sentence, use one word from the word bank and one phrase from the phrase bank.

Word Bank

short better best however low

Phrase Bank

go to school on my side form two lines
talk to my father open the door

1. ______________________________
____

2. ______________________________
____

3. ______________________________
____

NAME: ____

Directions: Read each sentence. Highlight the word from the word bank. Write the word on the line. Cut along the dotted lines to make cards. Staple or tape the cards together to make a book.

Word Bank				
hours	black	products	happened	whole

There were many products on the shelf.

____

Something great happened on the way to school.

____

I want to play the whole day.

____

It took three hours to get to the theme park.

____

The black bear ate the honey.

____

Recognize the Words

NAME: ____________________

Directions: Write the words from the word bank in alphabetical order. Then, write the words in reverse alphabetical order.

Word Bank				
hours	black	products	happened	whole

a b c d e f g h i j k l m n o p q r s t u v w x y z

Alphabetical Order

1. ____________________
2. ____________________
3. ____________________
4. ____________________
5. ____________________

Reverse Alphabetical Order

1. ____________________
2. ____________________
3. ____________________
4. ____________________
5. ____________________

NAME: ______________________________________

Directions: Cut out the letter tiles. Use them to make the words in the word bank. Glue the words on a separate sheet of paper.

Word Bank

hours black products happened whole

a	a	b	c	c
d	d	e	e	e
r	h	h	h	k
l	l	n	o	o
o	l	w	u	u
t	s	s	r	p
p	p			

Use the Words

NAME: ________________________________

Directions: Read the beginning of each sentence. Circle the word from the word bank. Then, use your imagination to write a creative ending.

Word Bank				
hours	black	products	happened	whole

1. I only eat products that ______________________

____

2. It took six hours to ______________________

____

3. Karen put on the black wig and ______________________

____

4. Because it happened so fast, I ______________________

____

5. The whole class began ______________________

____

NAME: ____________________

Directions: Use the cursive letters below to write each word three times. Make sure to connect the letters in each word.

a b c d e f g h i j k l m n
o p q r s t u v w x y z

example: each *each*

whole ____________________

____

happened ____________________

____

products ____________________

____

hours ____________________

____

____

black ____________________

____

____

Introduce the Words

NAME: ______________________________

Directions: Look at the picture in each box. Write the word from the word bank that goes with the picture. Cut out the cards. Punch a hole in each card and place it on your practice ring.

Word Bank

reached remember waves early measure

1. ______________________

2. ______________________

3. ______________________

4. ______________________

5. ______________________

NAME: ______________________________

Directions: Write each word three times. First, write the word in pencil. Next, write the word in crayon. Then, write the word in marker.

Word Bank

measure remember early waves reached

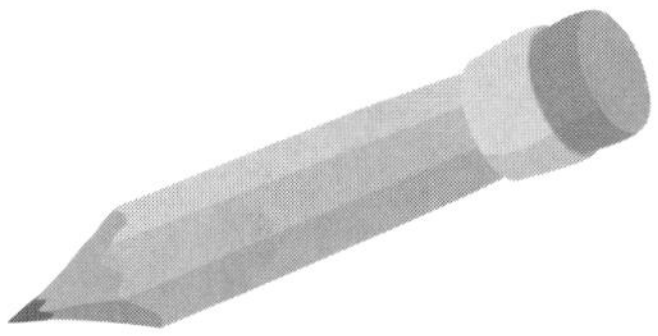	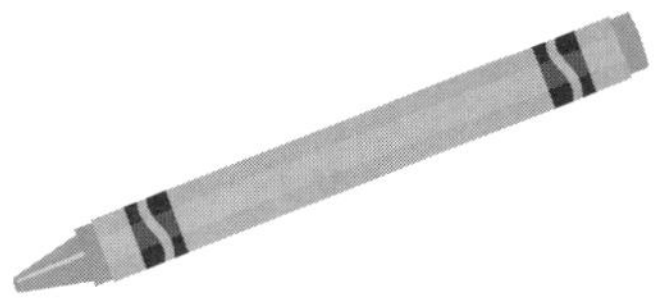	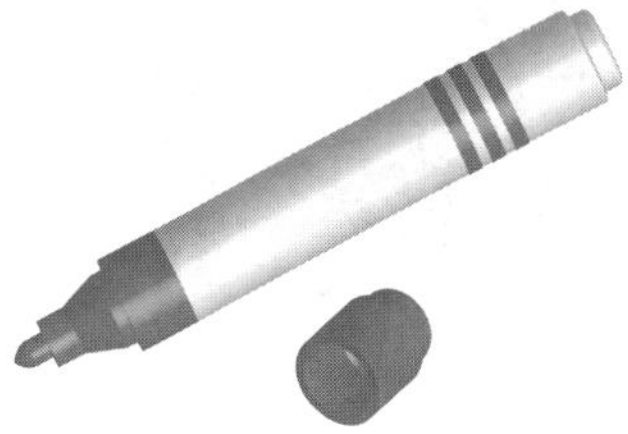

NAME: ______________________________

Directions: Find each letter on the telephone. For each letter, write the number that matches it. Add the numbers together. How much is each word?

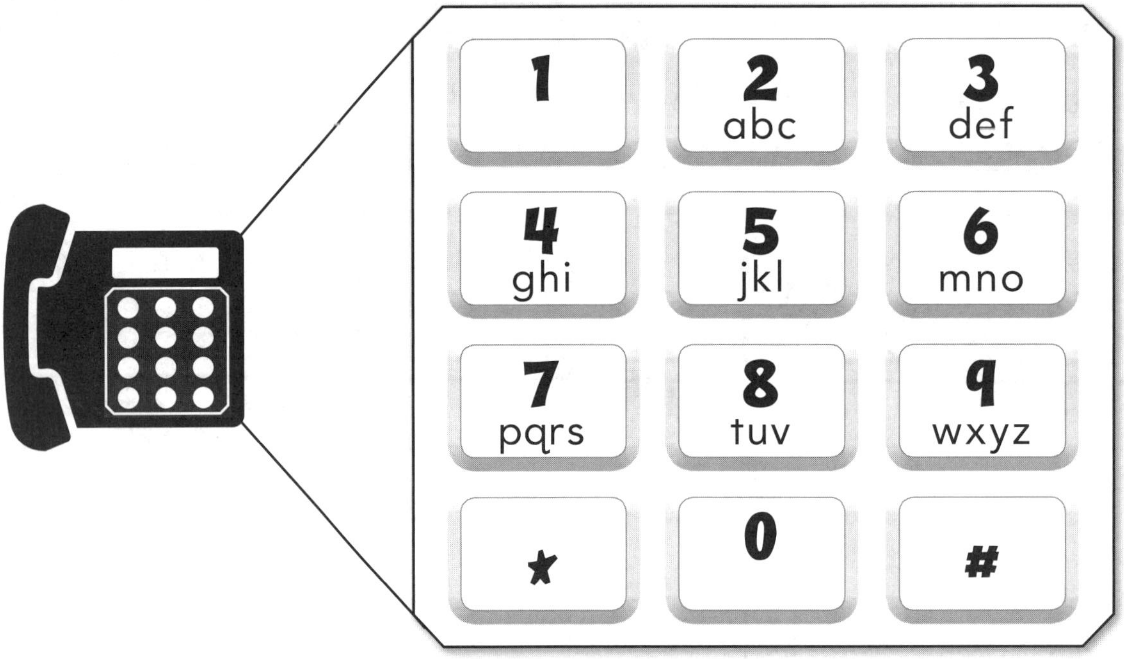

example: find 3 + 4 + 6 + 3 = 16

1. measure ______________________________

2. remember ______________________________

3. early ______________________________

4. waves ______________________________

5. reached ______________________________

Challenge: Which word has the highest value?

____

NAME: ____

Directions: Use the words and the code below to color in the image.

pink:	red:	yellow:	green:	brown:
measure	remember	early	waves	reached

NAME: ____________________

Directions: Pretend you are in the scene below and write a story about what is happening. Use as many words from the word bank as you can.

Word Bank

measure	remember	early	waves	reached

____

____

____

____

____

____

Challenge: Underline the words you used from the word bank, and read your story to a friend.

NAME: ______________________________

Directions: Write each word from the word bank one time. Next, color the words at the bottom of the page. Finally, cut along the dotted lines to create flash cards. Keep the cards in a folder to practice each day.

Word Bank

listen wind rock space covered

______________________ ______________________

______________________ ______________________

____

listen	
wind	rock
space	covered

NAME: ______________________________

Recognize the Words

Directions: Draw a square around the word **space**. Circle the word **rock**. Draw a triangle around the word **wind**. Draw a rectangle around the word **covered**. Underline word **listen**.

listen

covered

space

wind

space

wind

listen

rock

rock

listen

space

covered

wind

rock

covered

Challenge: Write each word twice in your own fun font.

1. ______________________________

2. ______________________________

3. ______________________________

4. ______________________________

5. ______________________________

NAME: ______________________________

Directions: Follow the directions below to play a memory game.

1. Cut apart the word cards below.
2. Place the cards facedown so you can't see the words.
3. Turn over one card, say the word, and spell it.
4. Turn over another card.
5. If the words are the same, keep the cards facing up.
6. If the words are different, turn the cards over and try again.
7. Continue playing until all the cards are facing up.

covered	listen	wind
covered	listen	wind
space	rock	rock
space		

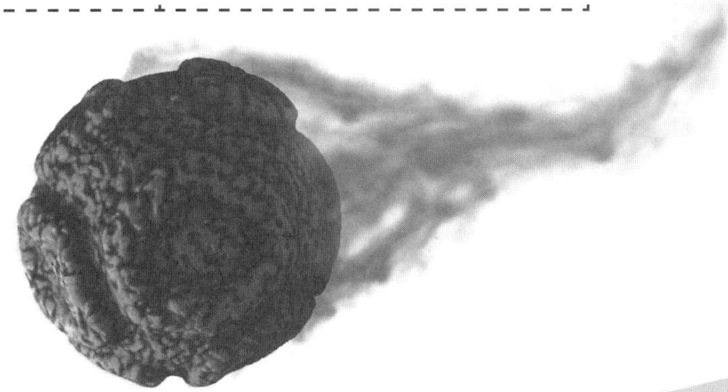

Use the Words

NAME: ____________________________________

Directions: Read the paragraph. Fill in each blank space with the best word from the word bank. Some words may be used more than once.

Word Bank				
listen	wind	rock	space	covered

Jason loves to go camping with his family. His job is to find a ________________________ for the campfire. He finds good wood, and puts it in a ________________________ between some rocks. Sometimes, the ________________________ makes it hard to keep the fire going, but Jason keeps it ________________________. He finds a big ________________________ to sit on, and he and his family ________________________ to each other tell stories.

Challenge: Which word did you use the most?

____

NAME: ______________________________

Directions: Write three sentences. In each sentence, use one word from the word bank and one phrase from the phrase bank.

Word Bank

listen wind rock space covered

Phrase Bank

near the sea stop the music under the earth
white clouds we left it here

1. ______________________________

____

2. ______________________________

____

3. ______________________________

____

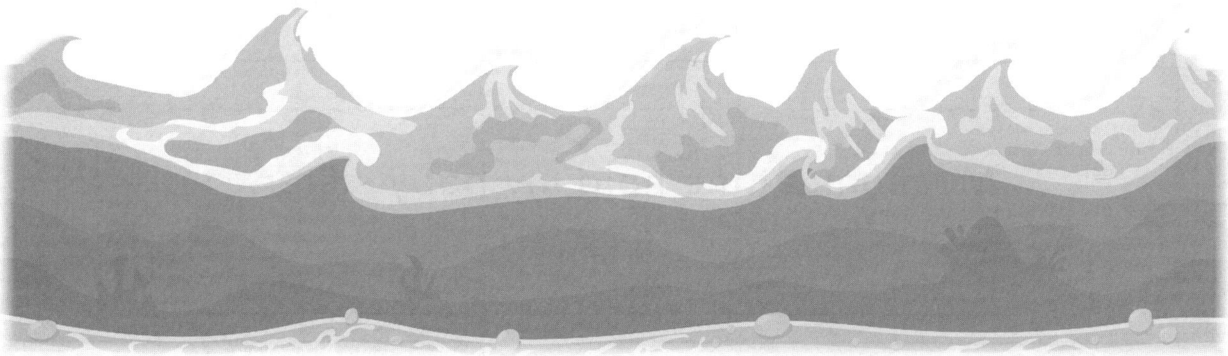

NAME: ____

Directions: Read each sentence. Highlight the word from the word bank. Write the word on the line. Cut along the dotted lines to make cards. Staple or tape the cards together to make a book.

Word Bank

fast several hold himself toward

The dog ran toward the tree.

____

Nathan walked home by himself.

____

The little squirrel ran really fast.

____

I checked out several books.

____

My mom let me hold my baby sister.

____

NAME: ____________________

Directions: Write the words from the word bank in alphabetical order. Then, write the words in reverse alphabetical order.

Word Bank

fast several hold himself toward

Alphabetical Order

1. ____________________
2. ____________________
3. ____________________
4. ____________________
5. ____________________

Reverse Alphabetical Order

1. ____________________
2. ____________________
3. ____________________
4. ____________________
5. ____________________

a b c d e f g h i j k l m n o p q r s t u v w x y z

NAME: ______________________________________

Directions: Cut out the letter tiles. Use them to make the words in the word bank. Glue the words on a separate sheet of paper.

Word Bank

fast several himself hold toward

a	a	a	d	d
e	e	e	f	w
f	h	h	i	l
l	l	m	o	o
r	r	s	s	s
t	t	v		

NAME: ______________________________

Directions: Read the beginning of each sentence. Circle the word from the word bank. Then, use your imagination to write a creative ending.

Word Bank				
fast	several	himself	hold	toward

1. He covered himself with ______________________

____

2. I will hold the ice cream ______________________

____

3. Several of my friends ______________________

____

4. He walked toward ______________________

____

5. She was running so fast that ______________________

____

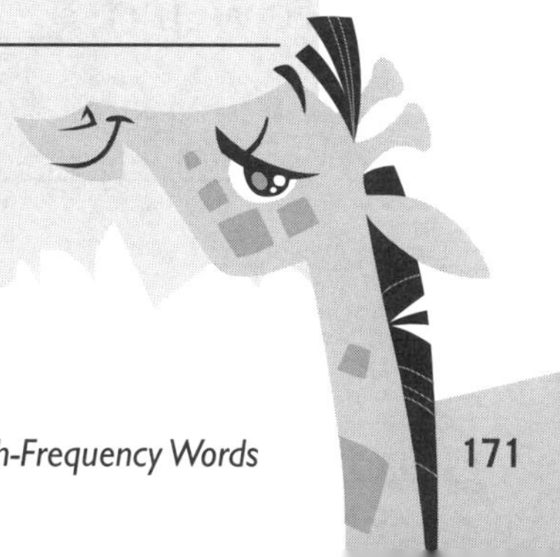

Write the Words

NAME: ______________________________

Directions: Use the cursive letters below to write each word three times. Make sure to connect the letters in each word.

a b c d e f g h i j k l m n
o p q r s t u v w x y z

example: letter *letter*

fast ______________________________

____

several ______________________________

____

himself ______________________________

____

hold ______________________________

____

____

toward ______________________________

____

____

NAME: ______________________________

Directions: Trace each word, then circle that word in the sentence. Cut along the dotted lines to make cards. Punch a hole in each card and place it on a practice ring.

five

There are five kids in my family.

step

Molly sat on the step to wait for her friends.

morning

I get out of bed every morning.

passed

Mark passed the ball to Alex.

vowel

The letter *u* is a vowel.

NAME: ______________________________

Directions: Write each word three times. First, write the word in pencil. Next, write the word in crayon. Then, write the word in marker.

Word Bank				
five	step	morning	passed	vowel

	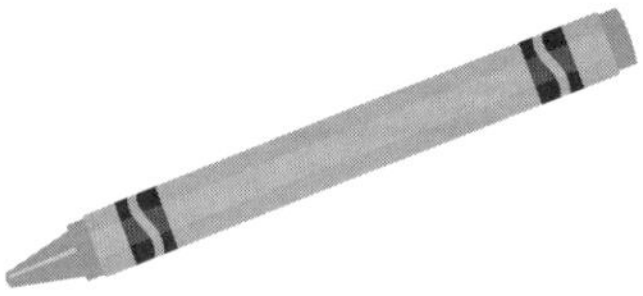	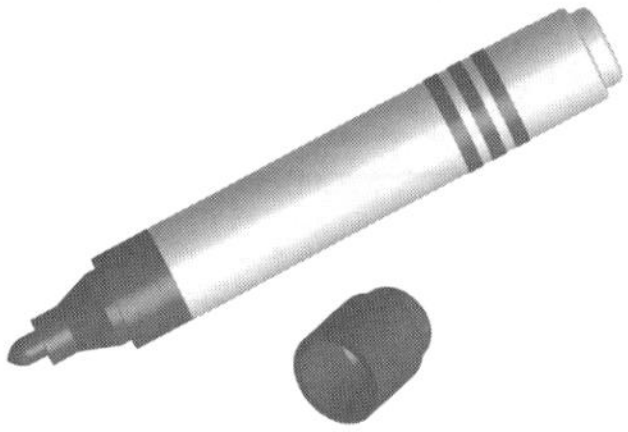

NAME: ______________________________

Directions: Find each letter on the telephone. For each letter, write the number that matches it. Add the numbers together. How much is each word?

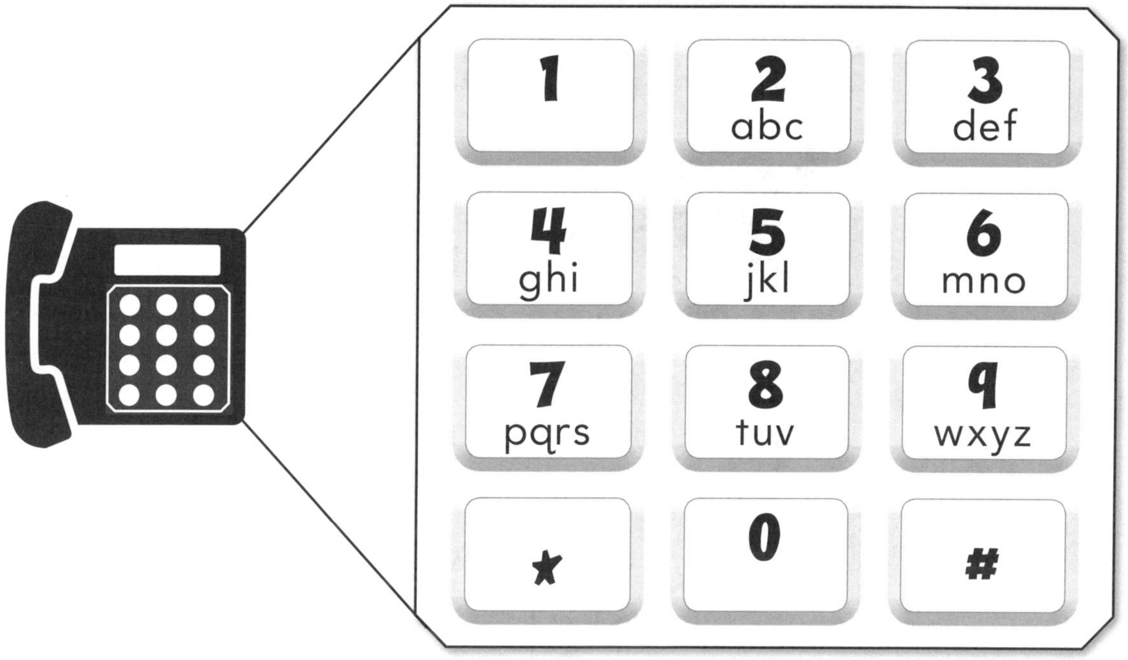

example: stand 7 + 8 + 2 + 6 + 3 = 26

1. five ______________________________

2. passed ______________________________

3. morning ______________________________

4. step ______________________________

5. vowel ______________________________

Challenge: Which word has the highest value?

____

Use the Words

NAME: ____

Directions: Use the words and the code below to color in the image.

red:	yellow:	blue:	brown:	black:
five	step	morning	passed	vowel

NAME: ______________________________________

Directions: Pretend you are in the scene below and write a story about what is happening. Use as many words from the word bank as you can.

Word Bank				
five	step	morning	passed	vowel

____

____

____

____

____

____

Challenge: Underline the words you used from the word bank, and read your story to a friend.

Introduce the Words

NAME: ____________________

Directions: Write each word from the word bank one time. Next, color the words at the bottom of the page. Finally, cut along the dotted lines to create flash cards. Keep the cards in a folder to practice each day.

Word Bank

true hundred against pattern numeral

____________________ ____________________

____________________ ____________________

____

true

against pattern

hundred numeral

NAME: ____

Directions: Draw a square around the word **true**. Draw a circle around the word **against**. Draw a triangle around the word **pattern**. Draw a rectangle around the word **hundred**. Underline the word **numeral**.

true pattern true

against

hundred numeral true

pattern

numeral numeral

hundred against

pattern against hundred

Challenge: Write each word twice in your own fun font.

1. ____

2. ____

3. ____

4. ____

5. ____

NAME: ____________________

Directions: Follow the directions below to play a memory game.

1. Cut apart the word cards below.
2. Place the cards facedown so you can't see the words.
3. Turn over one card, say the word, and spell it.
4. Turn over another card.
5. If the words are the same, keep the cards facing up.
6. If the words are different, turn the cards over and try again.
7. Continue playing until all the cards are facing up.

numeral	against	
numeral	against	
pattern	hundred	true
pattern	true	hundred

NAME: ______________________________

Directions: Read the paragraph. Fill in each blank space with the best word from the word bank. Some words may be used more than once.

Word Bank				
hundred	true	against	numeral	pattern

Sonia was learning Roman ______________s in school. Her teacher said the Roman ______________ for one ______________ is C. Sonia leaned ______________ her hand and looked confused. Her teacher explained that Roman ______________s are symbols that make a ______________, just like the digits we use to count to one ______________. Sonia didn't believe it was ______________, so the teacher showed her a picture.

Challenge: Which word did you use the most?

____

NAME: ____

Directions: Write three sentences. In each sentence, use one word from the word bank and one phrase from the phrase bank.

Word Bank

hundred | true | against | numeral | pattern

Phrase Bank

a long life | we got together | watch the game | too soon | next time

1. ____

____

2. ____

____

3. ____

____

NAME: ______________________________

Directions: Read each sentence. Highlight the word from the word bank. Write the word on the line. Cut along the dotted lines to make cards. Staple or tape the cards together to make a book.

Word Bank

table north slowly money map

How much money do I need to save?

____

The needle of the compass pointed north.

____

I set the table for our family dinner.

____

The turtle walked slowly toward the ocean.

____

We used the map to find the hidden treasure.

____

NAME: ____________________

Directions: Write the words from the word bank in alphabetical order. Then, write the words in reverse alphabetical order.

Word Bank

table north slowly money map

Alphabetical Order

1. ____________________
2. ____________________
3. ____________________
4. ____________________
5. ____________________

Reverse Alphabetical Order

1. ____________________
2. ____________________
3. ____________________
4. ____________________
5. ____________________

a b c d e f g h i j k l m n o p q r s t u v w x y z

NAME: ______________________________

Directions: Cut out the letter tiles. Use them to make the words in the word bank. Glue the words on a separate sheet of paper.

Word Bank

table north slowly money map

a	a	b	e	t
h	l	e	t	m
n	n	o	o	o
p	r	s	l	w
y	y	m		

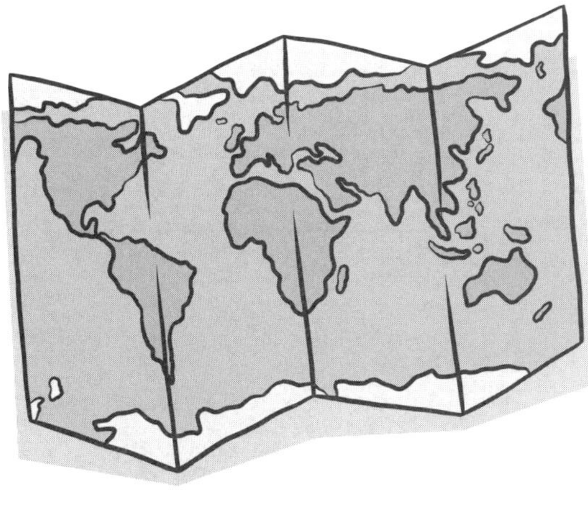

NAME: ____________________

Directions: Read the beginning of each sentence. Circle the word from the word bank. Then, use your imagination to write a creative ending.

Word Bank

north table slowly money map

1. On the map, X marks ____________________
____

2. The table legs ____________________
____

3. The boy slowly ____________________
____

4. Walk north until you ____________________
____

5. I gave all my money ____________________
____

NAME: ____________________

Directions: Use the cursive letters below to write each word three times. Make sure to connect the letters in each word.

a b c d e f g h i j k l m n
o p q r s t u v w x y z

example: three *three*

north ____________________

____

table ____________________

____

slowly ____________________

____

money ____________________

____

____

map ____________________

____

____

Introduce the Words

NAME: ______________________________

Directions: Look at the picture in each box. Write the word from the word bank that goes with the picture. Cut out the cards. Punch a hole in each card and place it on your practice ring.

Word Bank

farm	pulled	draw	voice	seen

1. ____________________

2. ____________________

3. ____________________

4. ____________________

5. ____________________

NAME: ____

Directions: Write each word three times. First write the word in pencil. Then, write the word in crayon. Lastly, write the word in marker.

Word Bank

farm pulled draw voice seen

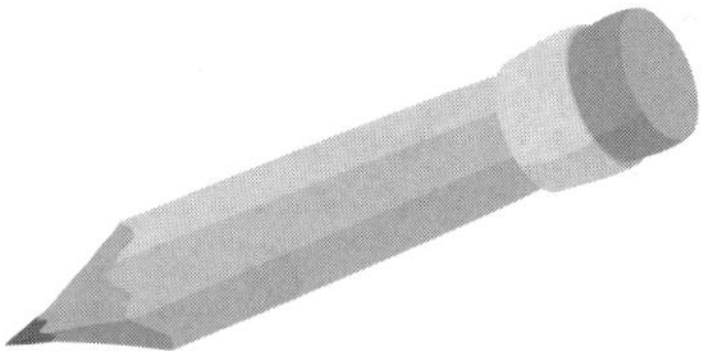	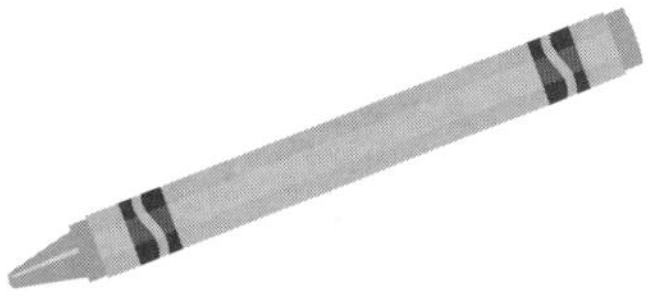	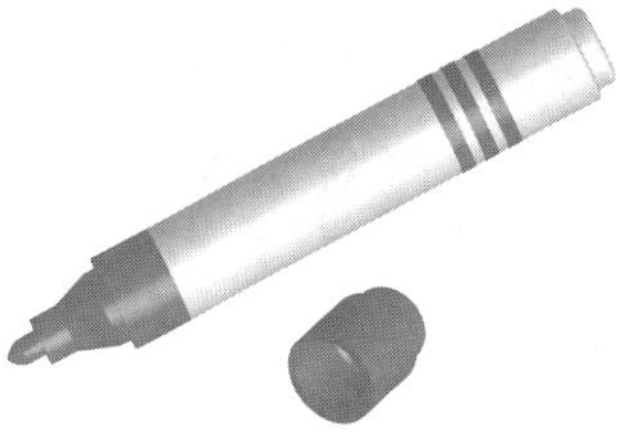

NAME: ______________________________

Directions: Find each letter on the telephone. For each letter, write the number that matches it. Add the numbers together. How much is each word?

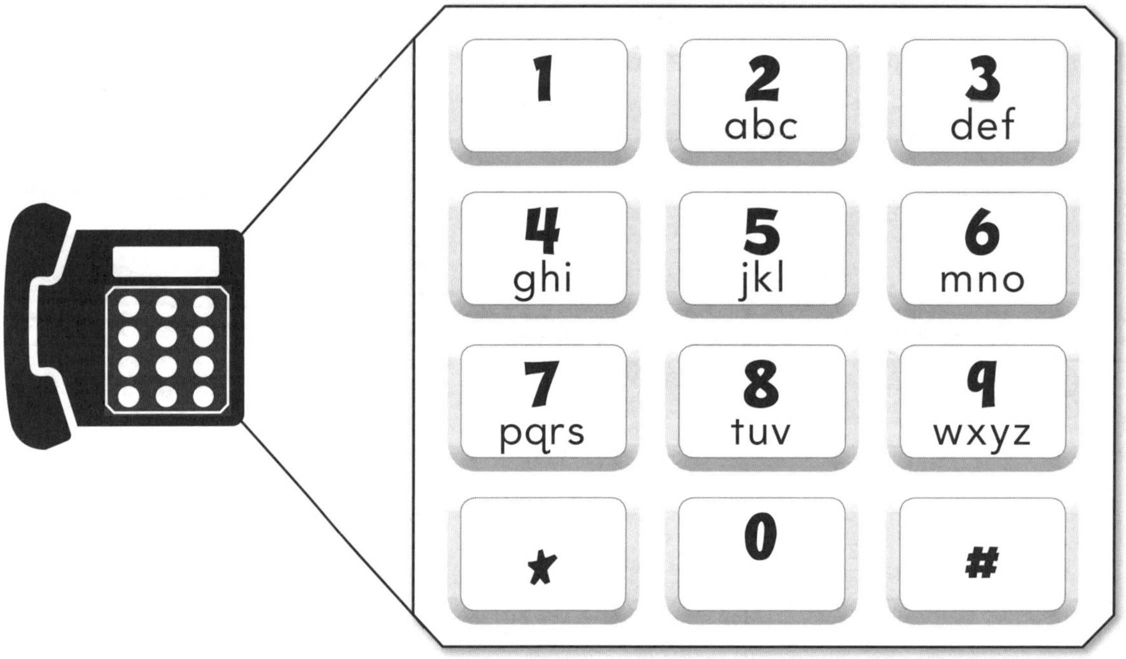

example: book <u>2 + 6 + 6 + 5 = 19</u>

1. farm ______________________________
2. pulled ______________________________
3. draw ______________________________
4. voice ______________________________
5. seen ______________________________

Challenge: Which word has the highest value?

____

NAME: ______________________________

Directions: Use the words and the code below to color in the image.

blue:	green:	brown:	red:	yellow:
pulled	draw	voice	farm	seen

Write the Words

NAME: ______________________________

Directions: Pretend you are in the scene below and write a story about what is happening. Use as many words from the word bank as you can.

Word Bank

farm	pulled	draw	voice	seen

____

____

____

____

____

____

Challenge: Underline the words you used from the word bank, and read your story to a friend.

ANSWER KEY

The activity pages that do not have specific answers to them are not included in this answer key. Students' answers will vary on these activity pages, so check that students are staying on task.

Week 1: Day 2 (page 14)

Week 1: Day 4 (page 16)

1. near
2. food
3. add
4. every
5. between

Week 2: Day 2 (page 19)

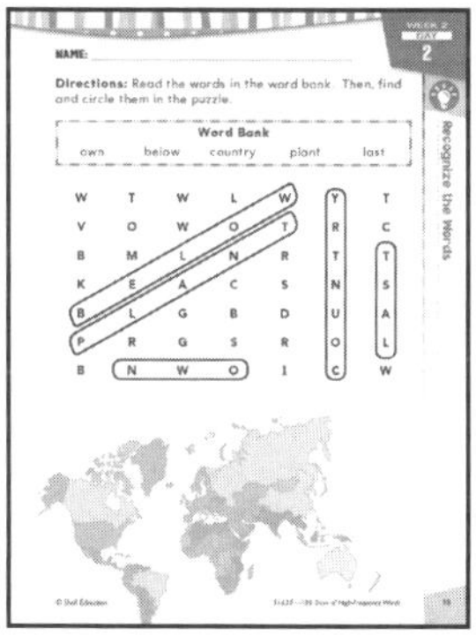

Week 2: Day 3 (page 20)

Forward/Backward

1. own	nwo
2. below	woleb
3. country	yrtnuoc
4. plant	tnalp
5. last	tsal

Uppercase/Lowercase

1. BELOW	below
2. COUNTRY	country
3. OWN	own
4. LAST	last
5. PLANT	plant

Week 2: Day 4 (page 21)

1. My family will **plant** trees in the spring.
2. I am going to visit another **country** this summer.
3. Juan can tie his **own** shoes!
4. We walked **below** the bridge in the park.
5. What is your first and **last** name?

Week 3: Day 1 (page 23)

1. father
2. keep
3. school
4. tree
5. never

Week 3: Day 2 (page 24)

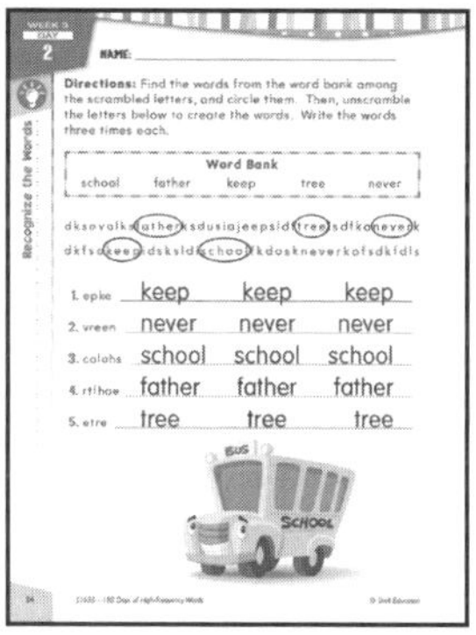

1. keep
2. never
3. school
4. father
5. tree

Week 3: Day 4 (page 26)

1. I like to **keep** my room clean.
2. A **school** of fish swam in the sea.
3. The **tree** in my yard fell during the hurricane.
4. I have to ask my **father** if I can go to the movie.
5. There are **never** 70 minutes in an hour.

Week 4: Day 2 (page 29)

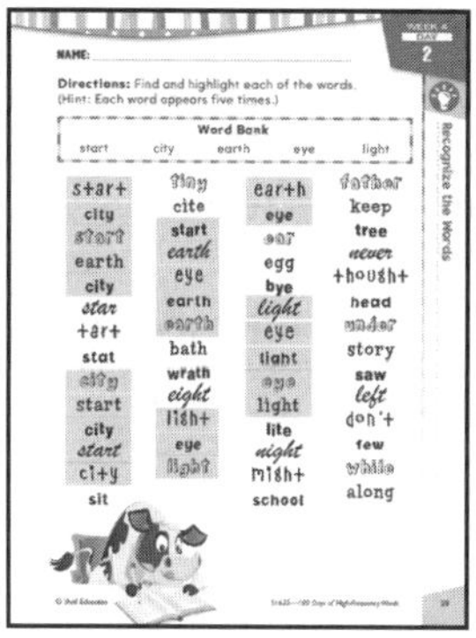

Week 4: Day 4 (page 31)

1. light
2. eye
3. city
4. start
5. earth

Week 5: Day 2 (page 34)

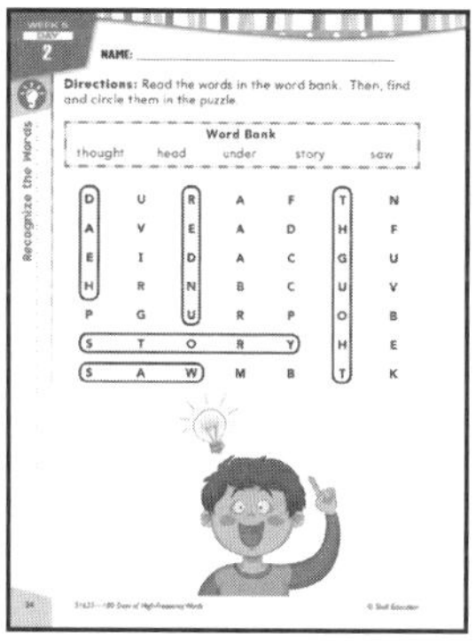

Week 5: Day 3 (page 35)

Forward/Backward

1. head	daeh
2. thought	thguoht
3. story	yrots
4. under	rednu
5. saw	was

Uppercase/Lowercase

1. THOUGHT	thought
2. UNDER	under
3. SAW	saw
4. HEAD	head
5. STORY	story

ANSWER KEY *(cont.)*

Week 5: Day 4 (page 36)

1. The teacher read the **story** to the class.
2. I hit my **head** on the monkey bars.
3. At the airport, Kim **saw** the plane land.
4. She **thought** it was going to rain.
5. Is the pencil **under** the chair?

Week 6: Day 1 (page 38)

1. while
2. Don't
3. left
4. few
5. along

Week 6: Day 2 (page 39)

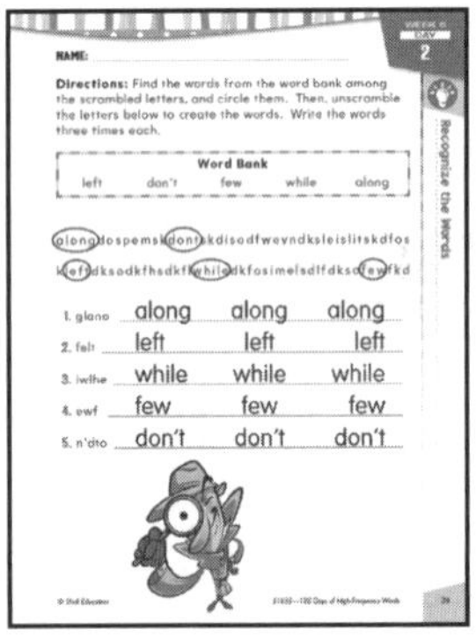
Word Bank: left, don't, few, while, along

1. glono along along along
2. felt left left left
3. iwlhe while while while
4. ewf few few few
5. n'dto don't don't don't

1. along
2. left
3. while
4. few
5. don't

Week 6: Day 4 (page 41)

1. I had to wait a **few** minutes for my mom.
2. She listened to music **while** she was working.
3. Come **along** with me to the store.
4. Father **left** the keys in the car.
5. I **don't** like to clean my room.

Week 7: Day 2 (page 44)

Word Bank: might, close, something, seem, next

Week 7: Day 4 (page 46)

1. seem
2. close
3. something
4. next
5. might

Week 8: Day 2 (page 49)

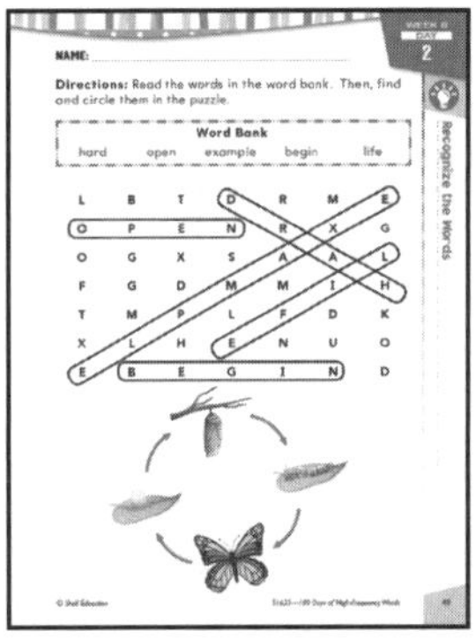
Word Bank: hard, open, example, begin, life

Week 8: Day 3 (page 50)

Forward/Backwards

1. hard drah
2. open nepo
3. example elpmaxe
4. begin nigeb
5. life efil

Uppercase/Lowercase

1. EXAMPLE example
2. OPEN open
3. HARD hard
4. LIFE life
5. BEGIN begin

Week 8: Day 4 (page 51)

1. The jar was **hard** to open.
2. The movie will **begin** in ten minutes.
3. I have lived in the country my whole **life**.
4. The gate to the backyard was left **open**.
5. I followed the **example** in the directions.

Week 9: Day 1 (page 53)

1. always
2. those
3. both
4. paper
5. together

Week 9: Day 2 (page 54)

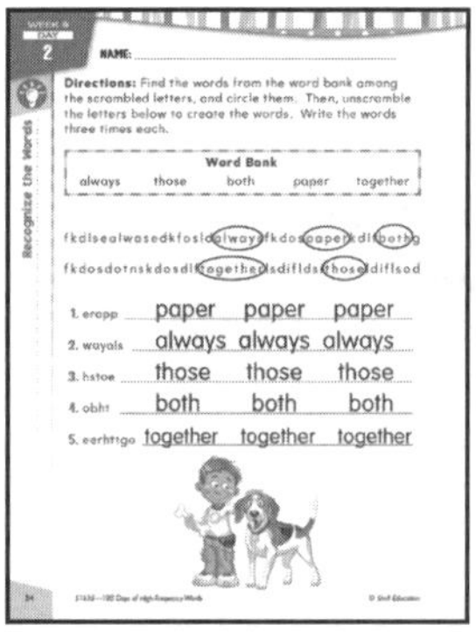
Word Bank: always, those, both, paper, together

1. eropp paper paper paper
2. wayals always always always
3. hstoe those those those
4. obht both both both
5. eerhtgo together together together

1. paper
2. always
3. those
4. both
5. together

Week 9: Day 4 (page 56)

1. Don't forget to write your name on the **paper**.
2. We like to play catch **together**.
3. The dog and cat are **both** sleeping.
4. You should **always** make your bed.
5. Would you like two of **those** cookies?

ANSWER KEY *(cont.)*

Week 10: Day 2 (page 59)

Week 10: Day 4 (page 61)

1. run
2. group
3. important
4. got
5. often

Week 11: Day 2 (page 64)

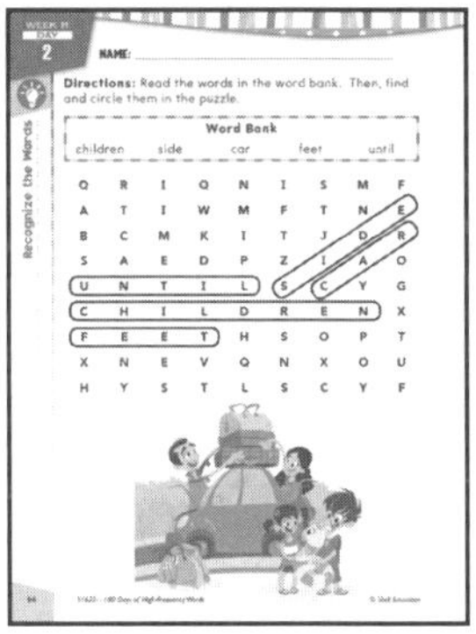

Week 11: Day 3 (page 65)

Forward/Backwards

1.	children	nerdlihc
2.	car	rac
3.	feet	teef
4.	side	edis
5.	until	litnu

Uppercase/Lowercase

1.	SIDE	side
2.	UNTIL	until
3.	CHILDREN	children
4.	CAR	car
5.	FEET	feet

Week 11: Day 4 (page 66)

1. There are four **children** in my family.
2. My uncle will pick me up in his **car.**
3. How many **feet** are in a mile?
4. I counted each **side** of the cube.
5. I waited **until** my mother came home.

Week 12: Day 1 (page 68)

1. walk
2. sea
3. night
4. mile
5. white

Week 12: Day 2 (page 69)

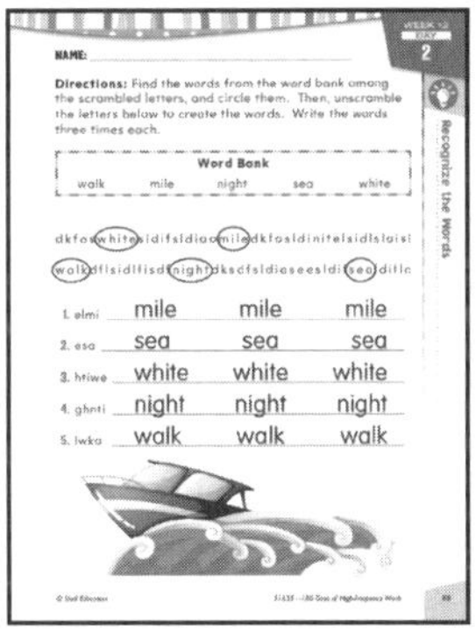

1. mile
2. sea
3. white
4. night
5. walk

Week 12: Day 4 (page 71)

1. Every **night**, the sun goes down.
2. The snow was cold and **white**.
3. Bill took a **walk** with his sister, Kate.
4. I can hear the **sea** from my bedroom window.
5. The school is one **mile** from my house.

Week 13: Day 2 (page 74)

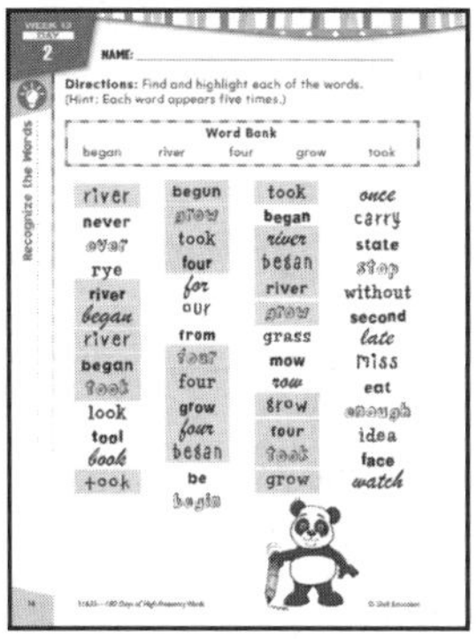

Week 13: Day 4 (page 76)

1. four
2. grow
3. river
4. began
5. took

Week 14: Day 2 (page 79)

Week 14: Day 3 (page 80)

Forward/Backwards

1.	hear	raeh
2.	book	koob
3.	state	etats
4.	once	ecno
5.	carry	yrrac

Uppercase/Lowercase

1.	ONCE	once
2.	HEAR	hear
3.	BOOK	book
4.	STATE	state
5.	CARRY	carry

ANSWER KEY *(cont.)*

Week 14: Day 4 (page 81)

1. My friend is moving to another **state.**
2. Do you **hear** that ringing noise?
3. I can play outside **once** I finish my dinner.
4. Can you help me **carry** this heavy box?
5. The **book** has sixteen chapters.

Week 15: Day 1 (page 83)

1. stop
2. second
3. without
4. late
5. miss

Week 15: Day 2 (page 84)

1. miss
2. without
3. stop
4. late
5. second

Week 15: Day 4 (page 86)

1. Do not leave **without** saying goodbye.
2. We learn addition facts in **second** grade.
3. Charlie didn't want to **miss** the movie.
4. She wanted me to **stop** playing the video game.
5. Hurry up, or we'll be **late** for school!

Week 16: Day 2 (page 89)

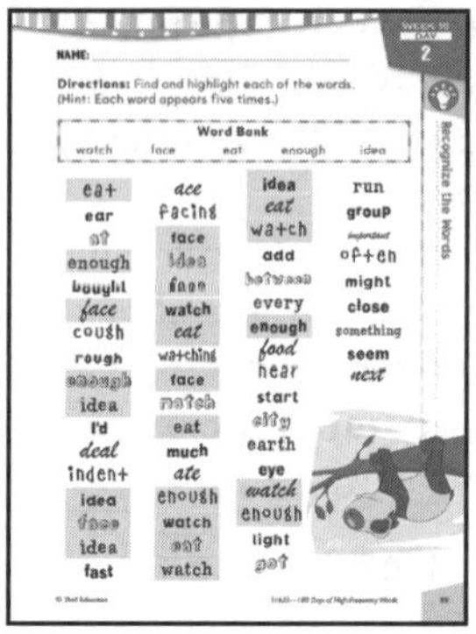

Week 16: Day 4 (page 91)

1. watch
2. enough
3. face
4. eat
5. idea

Week 17: Day 2 (page 94)

Week 17: Day 3 (page 95)

Forward/Backwards

1. far raf
2. cold dloc
3. real laer
4. let tel
5. almost tsomla

Uppercase/Lowercase

1. COLD cold
2. FAR far
3. ALMOST almost
4. LET let
5. REAL real

Week 17: Day 4 (page 96)

1. This winter will be very **cold**.
2. How **far** I can run in ten minutes?
3. John asked, "Did you **let** the dog out?"
4. Dad wasn't paying attention and **almost** missed the turn.
5. Todd wants a **real** goldfish for his birthday.

Week 18: Day 1 (page 98)

1. girl
2. above
3. sometimes
4. mountain
5. cut

Week 18: Day 2 (page 99)

1. mountain
2. above
3. sometimes
4. girl
5. cut

Week 18: Day 4 (page 101)

1. It took all day to hike up the **mountain** path.
2. The teacher showed us how to **cut** the paper.
3. **Sometimes**, my brother and I argue.
4. The **girl** bounced the big red ball nine times.
5. The tall man can see **above** the crowd.

ANSWER KEY *(cont.)*

Week 19: Day 2 (page 104)

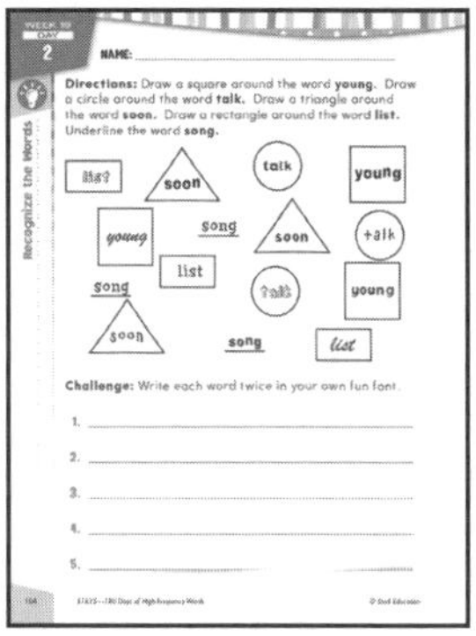
NAME:

Directions: Draw a square around the word **young**. Draw a circle around the word **talk**. Draw a triangle around the word **soon**. Draw a rectangle around the word **list**. Underline the word **song**.

Challenge: Write each word twice in your own fun font.

Week 19: Day 4 (page 106)

Haley's family will go shopping **soon**. Her mom is making a **list** of things to buy. On the drive to the store, Hayley's family will **talk** and sing a **song**. Her brother is too **young** to **talk** and sing the **song**. She hopes he will be able to **talk** and sing **soon**.

Challenge: talk

Week 20: Day 1 (page 108)

1. family
2. afternoon
3. leave
4. being
5. it's

Week 20: Day 2 (page 109)

Alphabetical Order

1. afternoon
2. being
3. family
4. it's
5. leave

Reverse Alphabetical Order

1. leave
2. it's
3. family
4. being
5. afternoon

Week 20: Day 4 (page 111)

1. leave
2. It's
3. being
4. family
5. afternoon

Week 21: Day 1 (page 113)

1. body
2. sun
3. stand
4. music
5. color

Week 21: Day 3 (page 115)

1. body $2 + 6 + 3 + 9 = 20$
2. sun $7 + 8 + 6 = 21$
3. music $6 + 8 + 7 + 4 + 2 = 27$
4. color $2 + 6 + 5 + 6 + 7 = 26$
5. stand $7 + 8 + 2 + 6 + 3 = 26$

Challenge: music

Week 22: Day 2 (page 119)

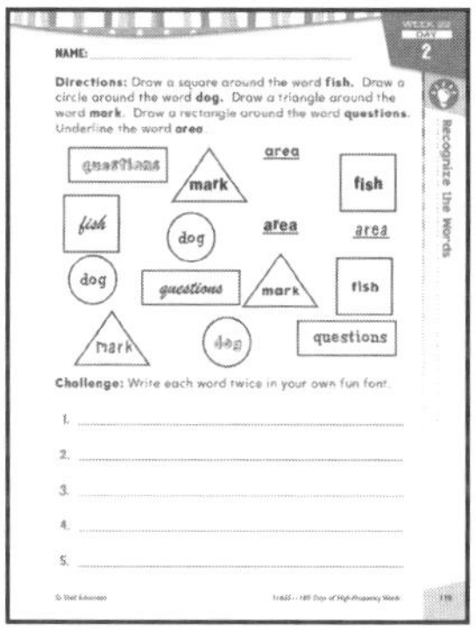
NAME:

Directions: Draw a square around the word **fish**. Draw a circle around the word **dog**. Draw a triangle around the word **mark**. Draw a rectangle around the word **questions**. Underline the word **area**.

Challenge: Write each word twice in your own fun font.

Week 22: Day 4 (page 121)

I can't have a pet **dog** because dogs make me sneeze. Dad took me to the pet store to buy a **fish** for a pet. The **fish** tank **area** was full of colorful **fish**. My dad had a lot of **questions** about taking care of **fish**. I picked a pretty yellow **fish** with a black **mark** on its tail.

Challenge: fish

Week 23: Day 1 (page 123)

1. birds
2. horse
3. room
4. problem
5. complete

Week 23: Day 2 (page 124)

Alphabetical Order

1. birds
2. complete
3. horse
4. problem
5. room

Reverse Alphabetical Order

1. room
2. problem
3. horse
4. complete
5. birds

Week 23: Day 4 (page 126)

1. birds
2. problem
3. complete
4. room
5. horse

Week 24: Day 3 (page 130)

1. knew $5 + 6 + 3 + 9 = 23$
2. since $7 + 4 + 6 + 2 + 3 = 22$
3. ever $3 + 8 + 3 + 7 = 21$
4. piece $7 + 4 + 3 + 2 + 3 = 19$
5. told $8 + 6 + 5 + 3 = 22$

Challenge: knew

Week 25: Day 2 (page 134)

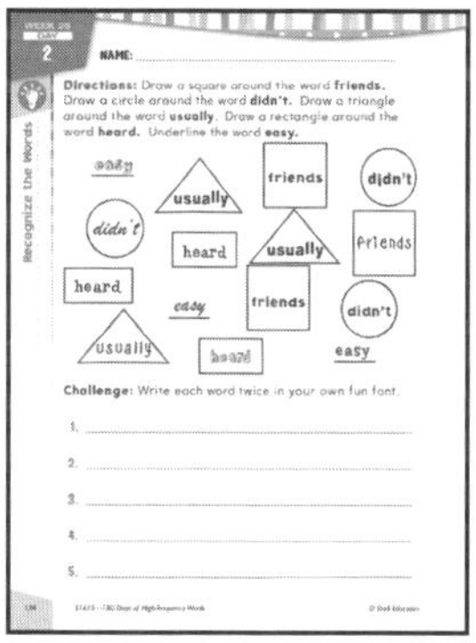
NAME:

Directions: Draw a square around the word **friends**. Draw a circle around the word **didn't**. Draw a triangle around the word **usually**. Draw a rectangle around the word **heard**. Underline the word **easy**.

Challenge: Write each word twice in your own fun font.

Week 25: Day 4 (page 136)

My **friends**, Jake and Amy, **usually** play with me after school. We like to play outside. It's fun and **easy** to think of things to do. On the radio, we **heard** it was going to rain all day. We **didn't** let the rain spoil our fun. Good **friends** can have fun playing inside, too.

Challenge: friends

Week 26: Day 1 (page 138)

1. order
2. red
3. become
4. sure
5. door

ANSWER KEY *(cont.)*

Week 26: Day 2 (page 139)

Alphabetical Order

1. become
2. done
3. order
4. red
5. sure

Reverse Alphabetical Order

1. sure
2. red
3. order
4. done
5. become

Week 26: Day 4 (page 141)

1. become
2. order
3. door
4. red
5. sure

Week 27: Day 1 (page 143)

1. across
2. top
3. during
4. today
5. ship

Week 27: Day 3 (page 145)

1. during
   3 + 8 + 7 + 4 + 6 + 4 = 32
2. across
   2 + 2 + 7 + 6 + 7 + 7 = 31
3. ship 7 + 4 + 4 + 7 = 22
4. top 8 + 6 + 7 = 21
5. today 8 + 6 + 3 + 2 + 9 = 28

Challenge: during

Week 28: Day 2 (page 149)

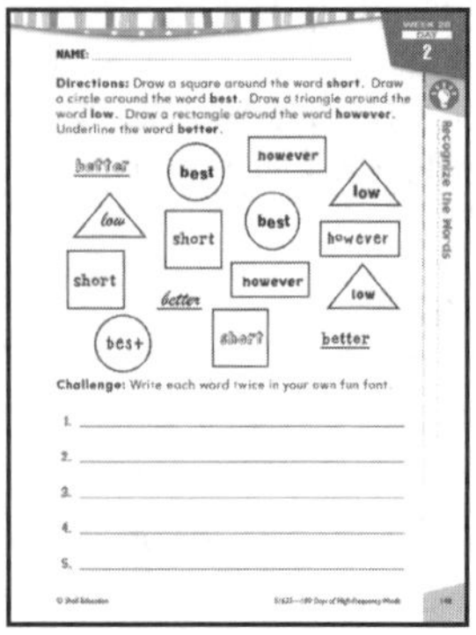

Week 28: Day 4 (page 151)

At the library, Jaden and Peter looked for **short** books. The librarian told them they could talk; **however**, they had to keep their voices **low**. Jaden read her book and whispered, "This is the **best** book ever!" In a **low** voice, Peter said his book was even **better**.

Challenge: low

Week 28: Day 5 (page 152)

1. It is a **short** walk when I **go to school**.
2. It is **better** to **form two lines**.
3. **Open the door however** you want to.
4. I sleep **best** when I'm **on my side**.
5. I **will talk to my father** in a **low** voice.

Week 29: Day 1 (page 153)

1. products
2. happened
3. whole
4. hours
5. black

Week 29: Day 2 (page 154)

Alphabetical Order

1. black
2. happened
3. hours
4. products
5. whole

Reverse Alphabetical Order

1. whole
2. products
3. hours
4. happened
5. black

Week 29: Day 4 (page 156)

1. products
2. hours
3. black
4. happened
5. whole

Week 30: Day 1 (page 158)

1. remember
2. measure
3. early
4. waves
5. reached

Week 30: Day 3 (page 160)

1. measure
   6 + 3 + 2 + 7 + 8 + 7 + 3 = 36
2. remember
   7 + 3 + 6 + 3 + 6 + 2 + 3 + 7 = 37
3. early 3 + 2 + 7 + 5 + 9 = 26
4. waves 9 + 2 + 8 + 3 + 7 = 29
5. reached
   7 + 3 + 2 + 2 + 4 + 3 + 3 = 24

Challenge: remember

Week 31: Day 2 (page 164)

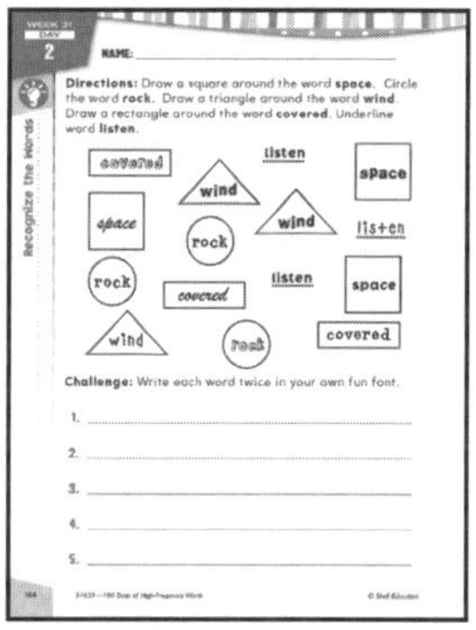

Week 31: Day 4 (page 166)

Jason loves to go camping with his family. His job is to find a **space** for the campfire. He finds wood and puts it in a **space** between some rocks. Sometimes, the **wind** makes it hard to keep the fire going, but Jason keeps it **covered.** He finds a big **rock** to sit on, and he and his family **listen** to each other tell stories.

Challenge: space

ANSWER KEY *(cont.)*

Week 31: Day 5 (page 167)

1. We **listen** to the waves **near the sea**.
2. The rocket shot through the **white clouds**, then into **space**.
3. I dug a hole and put the **rock under the earth**.
4. I said, "**Stop the music**!" as I **covered** my ears.
5. **We left it here**, but the **wind** blew it away.

Week 32: Day 1 (page 168)

1. toward
2. himself
3. fast
4. several
5. hold

Week 32: Day 2 (page 169)

Alphabetical Order

1. fast
2. himself
3. hold
4. several
5. toward

Reverse Alphabetical Order

1. toward
2. several
3. hold
4. himself
5. fast

Week 32: Day 4 (page 171)

1. himself
2. hold
3. several
4. toward
5. fast

Week 33: Day 3 (page 175)

1. five 8 + 4 + 8 + 3 = 18
2. passed
   7 + 2 + 7 + 7 + 3 + 3 = 29
3. morning
   6 + 6 + 7 + 6 + 4 + 6 + 4 = 39
4. step 7 + 8 + 3 + 7 = 25
5. vowel 8 + 6 + 9 + 3 + 5 = 31

Challenge: morning

Week 34: Day 2 (page 179)

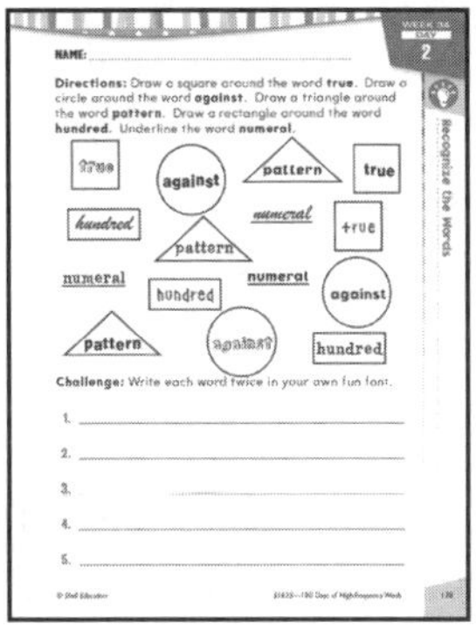
WEEK 34 DAY 2

NAME:

Directions: Draw a square around the word **true**. Draw a circle around the word **against**. Draw a triangle around the word **pattern**. Draw a rectangle around the word **hundred**. Underline the word **numeral**.

true against pattern true
hundred numeral true
pattern
numeral hundred numeral against
pattern against hundred

Challenge: Write each word twice in your own fun font.

1.
2.
3.
4.
5.

Recognize the Words

Week 34: Day 4 (page 181)

Sonia was learning Roman numerals in school. Her teacher said the Roman **numeral** for one **hundred** is C. Sonia leaned **against** her elbow and looked confused. Her teacher explained that Roman **numerals** are symbols that make a **pattern**, just like the digits we use to count to one **hundred**. Sonia didn't believe it was **true**, so the teacher showed her a picture.

Challenge: pattern

Week 34: Day 5 (page 182)

1. The man lived **a long life** until he was one **hundred**.
2. **We got together** and made a Roman **numeral** X with chalk.
3. Lean **against** the tree and **watch the game**.
4. It is **true** that I left **too soon**.
5. **Next time**, we will make a **pattern** out of the blocks.

Week 35: Day 1 (page 183)

1. money
2. north
3. table
4. slowly
5. map

Week 35: Day 2 (page 184)

Alphabetical Order

1. map
2. money
3. north
4. slowly
5. table

Reverse Alphabetical Order

1. table
2. slowly
3. north
4. money
5. map

Week 35: Day 4 (page 186)

1. map
2. table
3. slowly
4. north
5. money

Week 36: Day 1 (page 188)

1. pulled
2. voice
3. draw
4. seen
5. farm

Week 36: Day 3 (page 190)

1. farm 3 + 2 + 7 + 6 = 18
2. pulled
   7 + 8 + 5 + 5 + 3 + 3 = 31
3. draw 3 + 7 + 2 + 9 = 21
4. voice 8 + 6 + 4 + 2 + 3 = 23
5. seen 7 + 3 + 3 + 6 = 19

Challenge: pulled

HOME/SCHOOL CONNECTIONS AND EXTENSION ACTIVITIES

Pages 200–207 can be used as home/school connection activities for additional practice or classroom extension activities. All game sheets have been left blank so the teacher can differentiate for each individual student and/or group in the class. The flash cards on pages 209–215 can be used as game cards, as well as student-facing assessment cards for quarterly assessments.

BINGO

Write the high-frequency words of the week (or ones that need to be practiced) on the BINGO board. Select a word from the deck of flash cards. Any player who has the word can place a chip on it. The first player to make a straight line calls out "Bingo!"

		FREE SPACE		

HOME/SCHOOL CONNECTIONS AND EXTENSION ACTIVITIES *(cont.)*

Race to 20! Race to 30!

Give each student a whiteboard or note pad to serve as a scoreboard. Use the flash cards from pages 208–215 to create a card pile for this game. Pick a card from the flash card pile, read the word, and count the letters in the word. Add a tally mark for each letter. Take turns picking cards, reading words, and adding up tally marks. The first player to reach 20 tally marks wins! As a challenge, Race to 30!

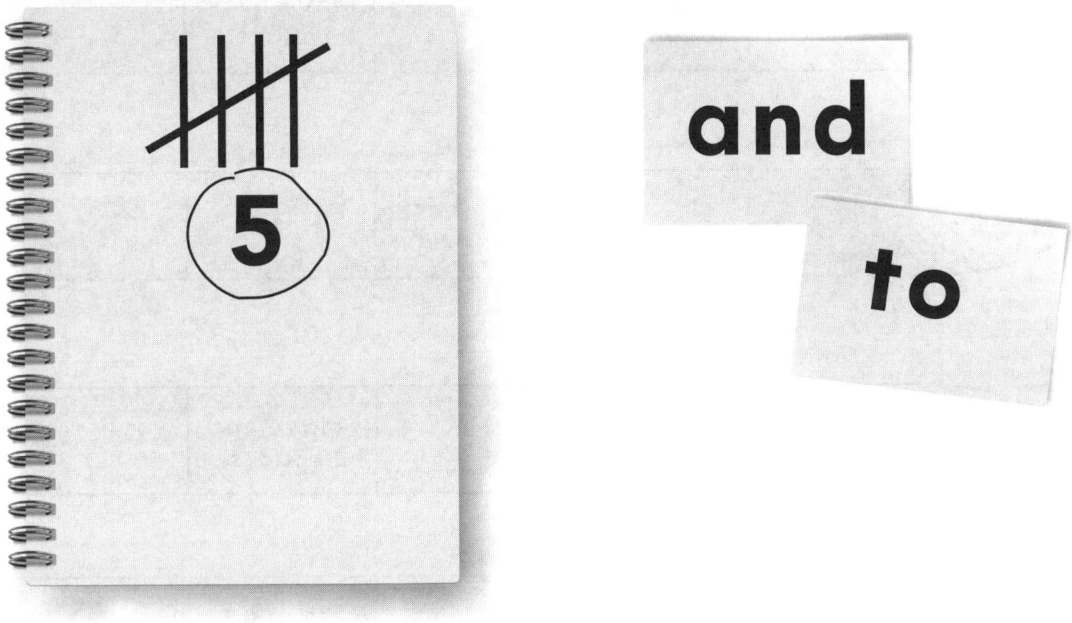

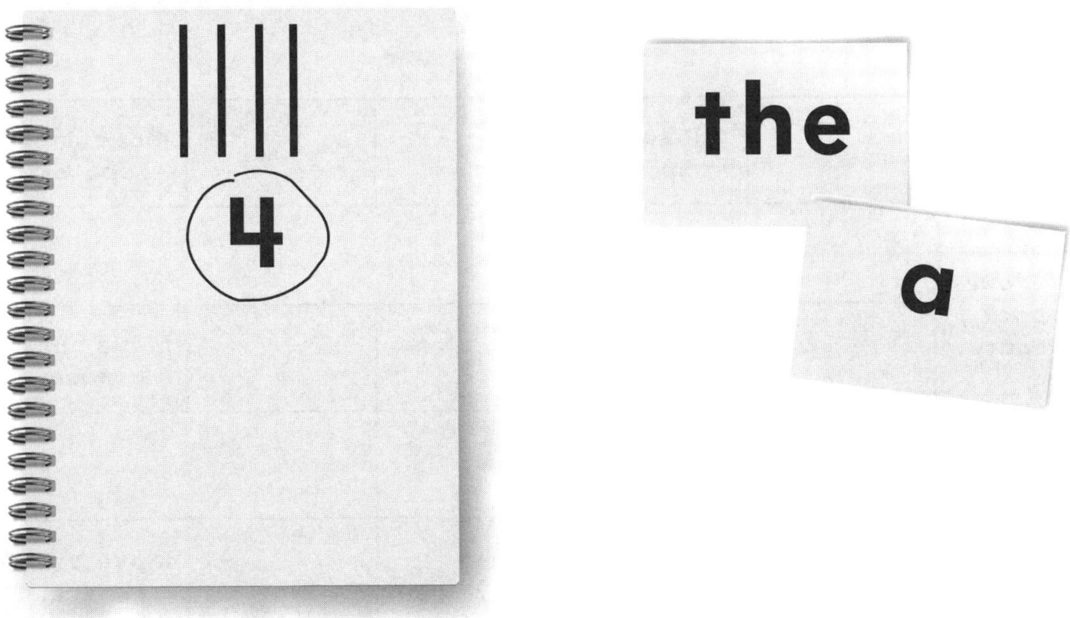

HOME/SCHOOL CONNECTIONS AND EXTENSION ACTIVITIES *(cont.)*

Word Board Game

Choose several words and place those flash cards in a pile. Write the words multiple times on the game board until all spaces are filled. Then, distribute a chip to each player. Have each player select a flash card, count the number of letters in the word, and then move his or her chip that number of spaces. Have students read every space they land on. The first player to reach the finish line wins!

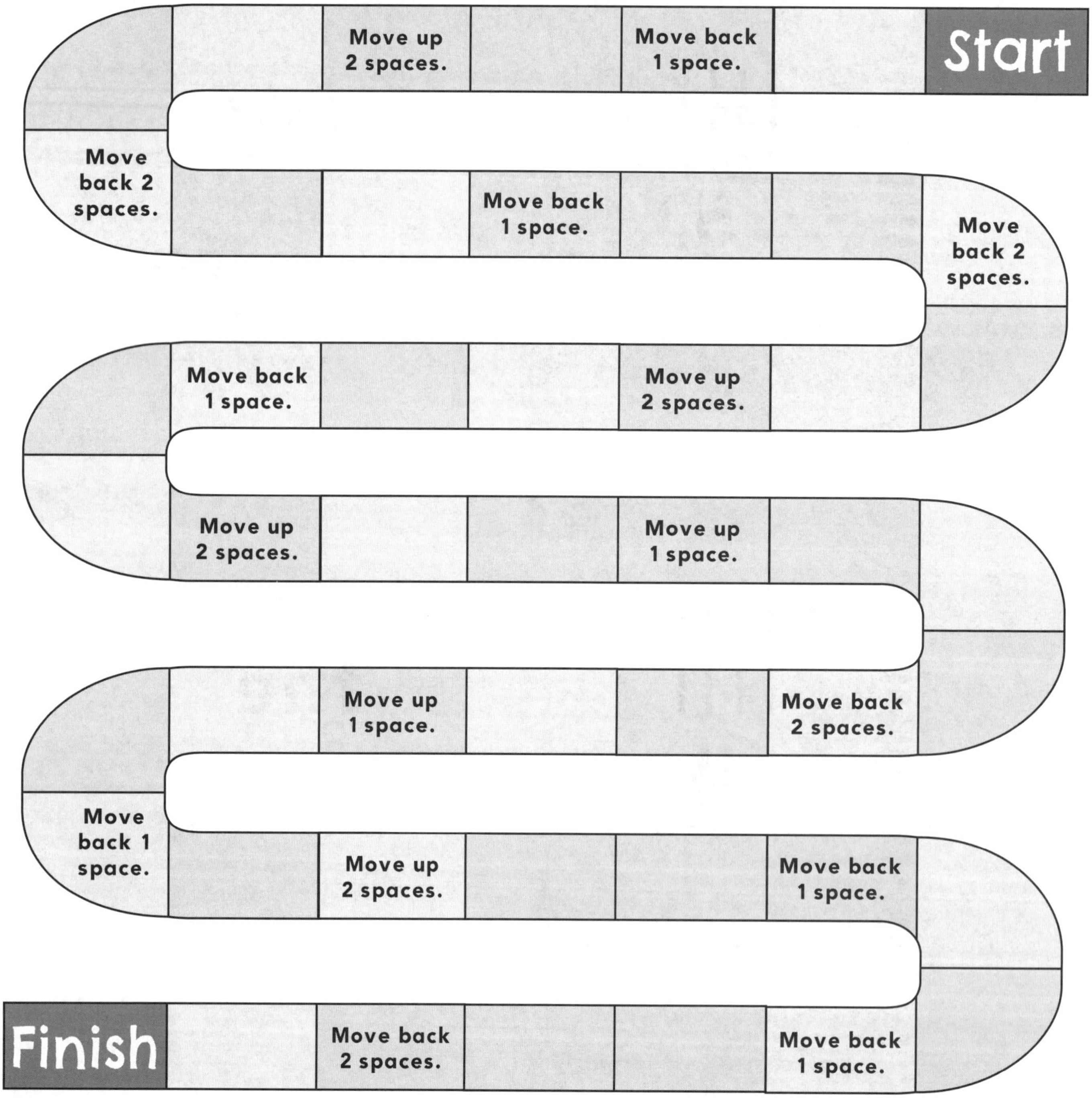

HOME/SCHOOL CONNECTIONS AND EXTENSION ACTIVITIES *(cont.)*

Word Bar Graph

Write the words of the week multiple times in the spinner. Write the words of the week on the lines at the bottom of the graph.

Use a paper clip and pencil to make a pointer. Place the paper clip in the middle of the spinner. Put the pencil inside of the paper clip so when it is spun, the paper clip circles around the pencil.

Have each student spin the pointer and read the word that the paper clip lands on. Starting from the box above the word, fill in one box each time the pointer lands on that word. Play until one column reaches the top.

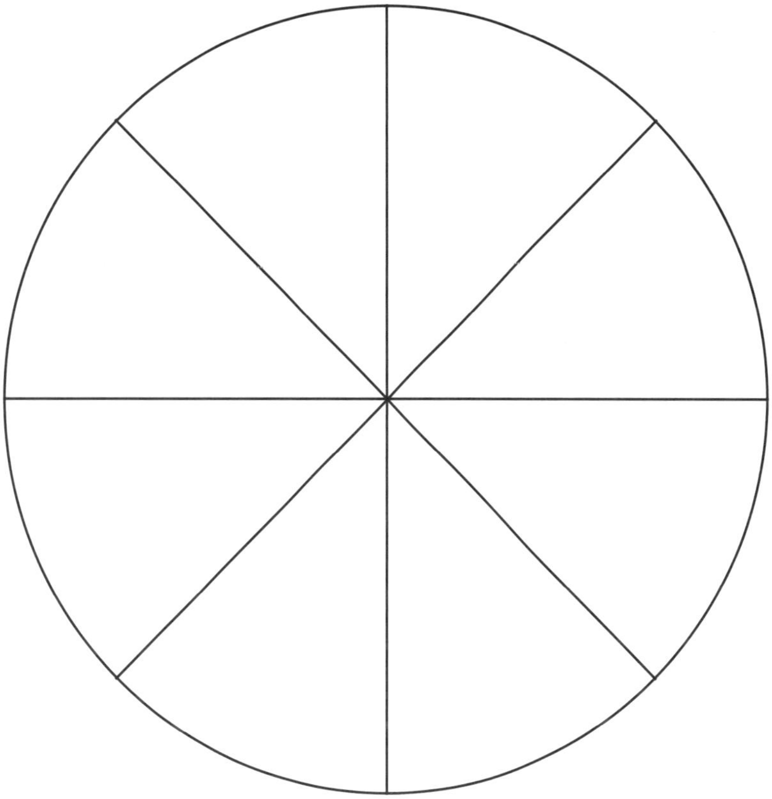

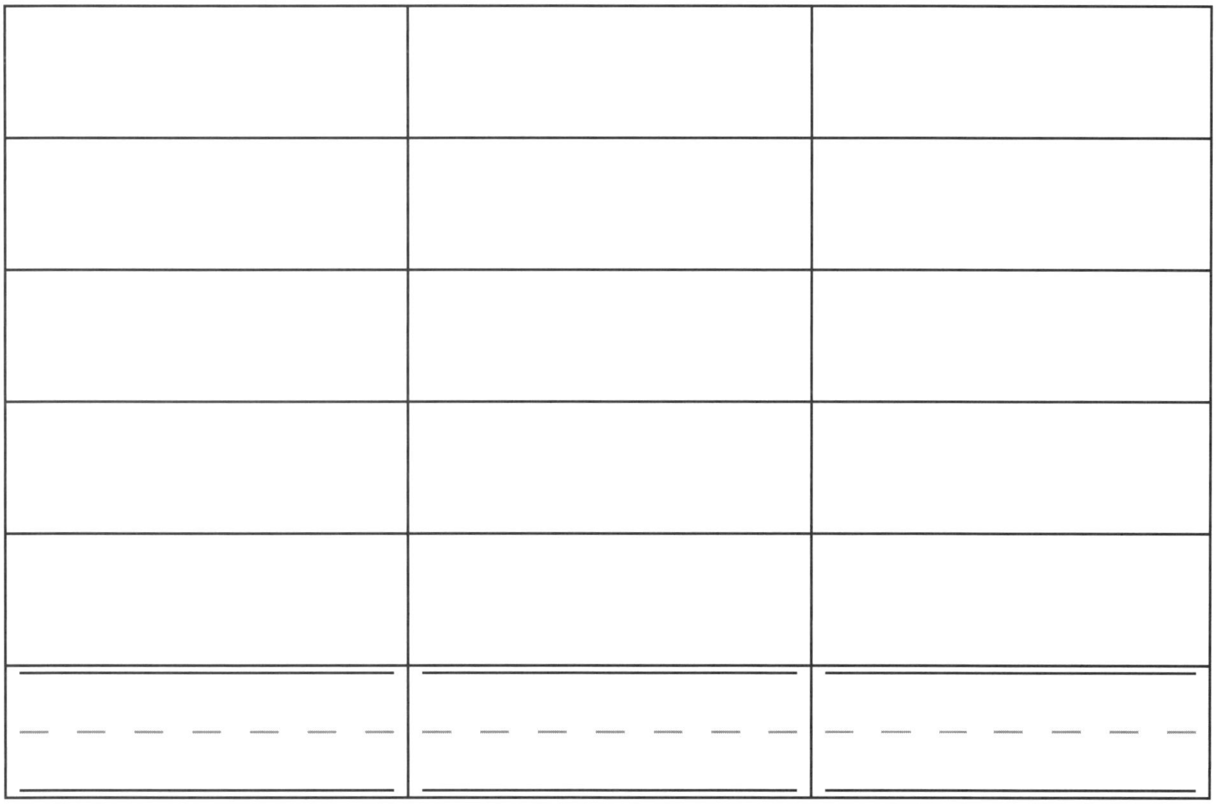

HOME/SCHOOL CONNECTIONS AND EXTENSION ACTIVITIES *(cont.)*

Tally It Up!

Select six words, and write them in the second column. Have each student roll a die 20 times. For each roll, students say the word associated with each number, then color one tally mark. For each roll have students color one box next to the word that matches the number rolled. To liven up the game, instruct students to say each word in a normal voice and a strange one.

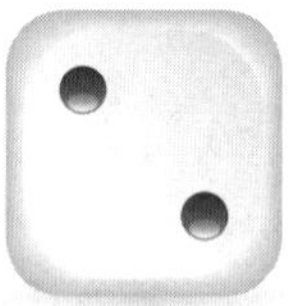									
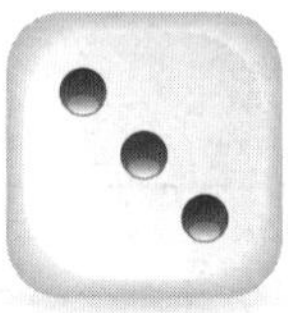									
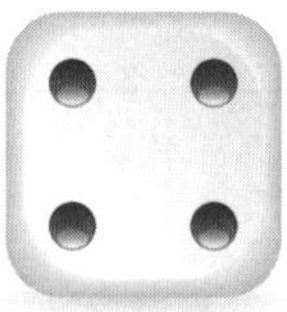									

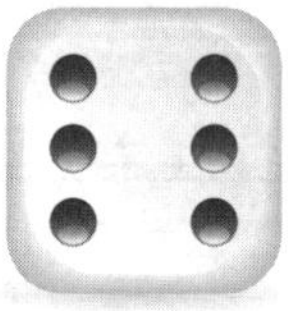									

HOME/SCHOOL CONNECTIONS AND EXTENSION ACTIVITIES *(cont.)*

Scavenger Hunt for the Print Rich Classroom

Have students take a classroom walk to find some of the words. When students find a word have them stand next to it. This game can be differentiated to include the following hunts:

- Find a word in the classroom that starts with the same sound as . . .
- Find a word in the classroom that ends with the same sound as . . .
- Find a word in the classroom that starts/ends with the same letter as . . .
- Find a word in the classroom that has the same syllable count as . . .
- Find a word in the classroom that has the same amount of letters as . . .
- Find a word in the classroom that has the same amount of vowels/consonants as . . .

Tiny-Print Word Search

Use the chart below to find the high-frequency words of the week. Give each student a magnifying glass. Use the list on page 11 to call out each high-frequency word. **Note:** All of the words in this book are listed below multiple times!

few	last	story	plant	earth	got	add	important	story	city	start	near	country	between	side
book	few	head	example	river	feet	thought	along	often	start	began	next	took	begin	children
every	own	keep	life	those	walk	left	father	took	next	close	keep	life	state	almost
since	horse	room	birds	problem	knew	mark	knew	told	complete	usually	piece	room	piece	dog
carry	seem	open	paper	last	real	tree	hear	head	something	walk	river	together	hear	without
hard	below	food	car	mile	group	while	light	carry	got	family	miss	own	idea	cold
afternoon	area	sun	body	dog	horse	color	ever	complete	fish	usually	question	ever	told	stand
seen	rock	morning	early	hundred	vowel	pattern	draw	voice	map	toward	seen	space	several	early
city	hard	until	left	saw	above	never	without	paper	eye	until	while	real	cut	sometimes
today	heard	ever	order	didn't	order	short	ship	door	usually	become	ship	across	top	short
watch	school	might	grow	four	family	along	group	almost	night	add	grow	let	eye	white
cold	begin	late	feet	between	face	don't	enough	might	always	mountain	mile	mountain	example	stop
fast	table	pulled	several	hold	passed	north	step	remember	numeral	draw	voice	north	money	pattern
thought	earth	children	together	second	girl	every	never	let	under	soon	tree	being	young	late
list	those	near	state	side	leave	close	idea	sometimes	sea	seem	soon	second	song	young
being	light	began	book	eat	list	saw	always	don't	both	cut	open	something	leave	almost
below	father	run	night	both	once	country	eat	plant	white	talk	song	school	under	girl
talk	often	stop	miss	once	four	car	far	watch	important	face	run	enough	far	sea
mark	stand	question	it's	since	birds	afternoon	fish	color	music	sun	music	problem	area	body
complete	afternoon	fish	music	afternoon	question	stand	music	area	sun	body	color	birds	problem	body
sun	area	mark	question	fish	it's	dog	stand	problem	color	mark	told	complete	birds	dog
easy	since	become	room	piece	heard	horse	usually	knew	easy	since	sure	piece	room	door
top	didn't	during	friends	during	told	friends	sure	ever	red	across	red	horse	today	knew
hours	short	best	however	short	black	better	best	however	better	low	black	low	hours	products
passed	products	whole	covered	hold	measure	remember	space	wind	happened	reached	waves	wind	rock	listen
whole	waves	true	five	happened	covered	morning	against	himself	vowel	numeral	step	true	against	himself
table	slowly	measure	toward	farm	hundred	map	listen	slowly	fast	pulled	money	farm	reached	five

HOME/SCHOOL CONNECTIONS AND EXTENSION ACTIVITIES *(cont.)*

Guess my Word

Print the flash cards on pages 208–215. Have students work in pairs. One partner should hold a flash card to his or her forehead while the other partner gives the clues. Once the partner guesses the word correctly, the other student takes a turn. Students can use any of the prompts below as clues:

- Use the word in a sentence, for example "I went to _______ party."
- "The word has _____ syllables."
- "The word rhymes with ______."
- "The word has _____ vowels."
- "The word has ____ consonants."

Dance and Write

Give every pair of students a dry-erase board and marker. Play some music. When the music stops, call out a word. The first team to write the word on their board and hold it up gets the point.

Dance, Tally, and Graph

As an alternative to Dance and Write, remove the competitive aspect. Give every student a clipboard and a sheet of paper. Have students write the words of the week on their paper. Play music, and when the music stops call out a word. Have students write a tally mark next to every word called. When students reach five tally marks for every word, repeat the game/song.

HOME/SCHOOL CONNECTIONS AND EXTENSION ACTIVITIES *(cont.)*

Ice Cream Word Sort

Choose a sorting category for students, and write it on the cone. Using the flash cards from pages 208–215, have students select and write words that fit the sort onto each scoop of ice cream. Have students color the ice cream once complete. Sorting categories can be found on pages 205–206.

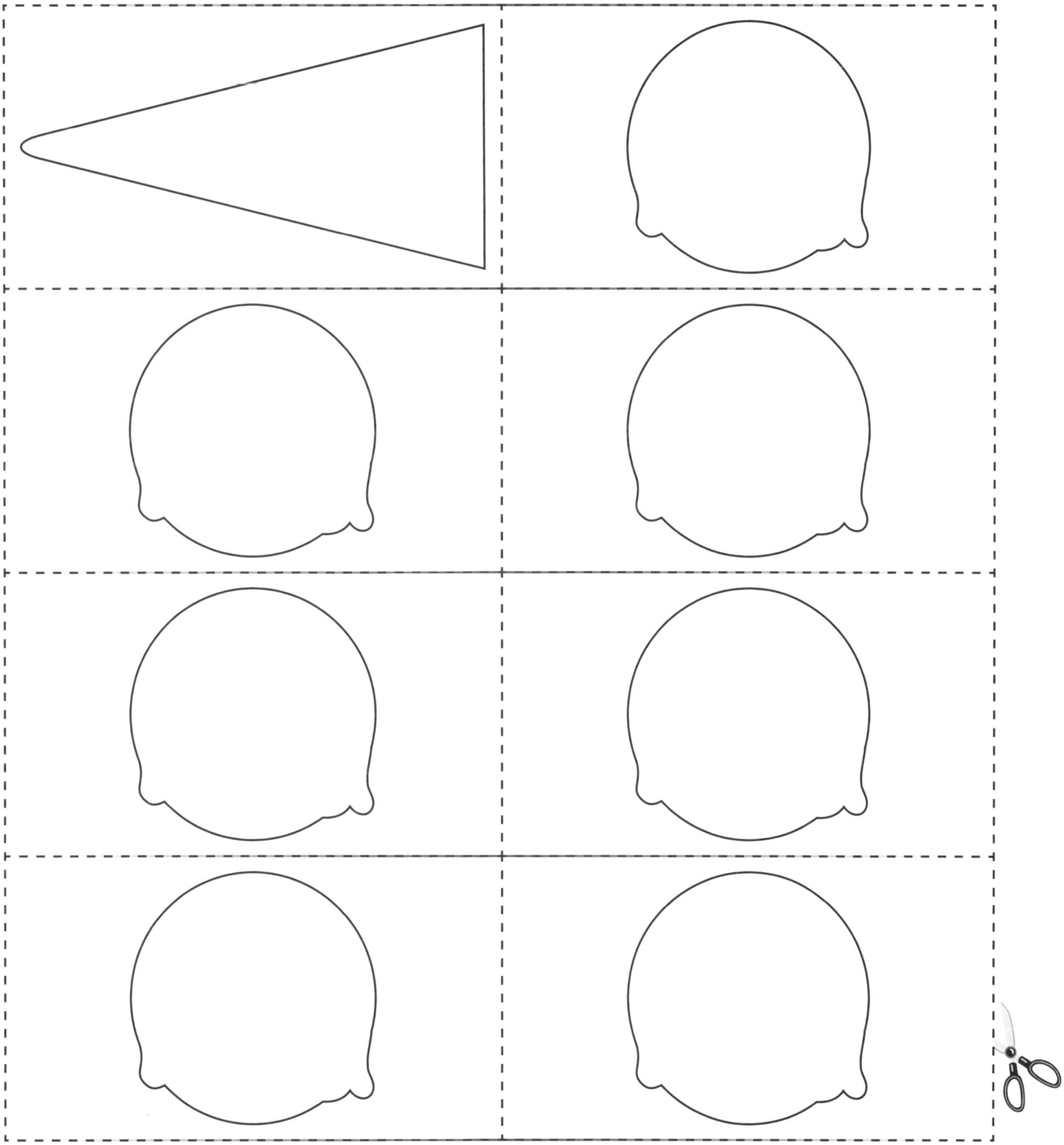

HIGH-FREQUENCY WORDS FLASH CARDS

The flash cards on pages 208–215 are organized by week. **Note:** If you are using the cards for the student diagnostic assessment, have students read the words left to right, as they would read text in a book. Below you will find weeks 1–4.

near	last	never	light
food	plant	tree	eye
every	country	keep	earth
between	below	father	city
add	own	school	start

HIGH-FREQUENCY WORDS FLASH CARDS *(cont.)*

Below you will find weeks 5–8.

saw	along	next	life
story	while	something	begin
under	few	seem	example
head	don't	close	open
thought	left	might	hard

HIGH-FREQUENCY WORDS FLASH CARDS *(cont.)*

Below you will find weeks 9–12.

together	often	until	sea
paper	important	feet	white
both	group	car	walk
those	run	side	night
always	got	children	mile

HIGH-FREQUENCY WORDS FLASH CARDS *(cont.)*

Below you will find weeks 13–16.

grow	state	miss	watch
began	carry	late	face
four	once	second	idea
took	hear	without	enough
river	book	stop	eat

HIGH-FREQUENCY WORDS FLASH CARDS *(cont.)*

Below you will find weeks 17–21.

almost	cut	song	afternoon	sun
let	mountain	list	it's	stand
cold	girl	soon	family	color
far	sometimes	talk	leave	music
real	above	young	being	body

HIGH-FREQUENCY WORDS FLASH CARDS *(cont.)*

Below you will find weeks 22–26.

dog	room	told	heard	order
mark	complete	piece	easy	red
area	birds	ever	friends	door
fish	horse	since	didn't	become
question	problem	knew	usually	sure

HIGH-FREQUENCY WORDS FLASH CARDS *(cont.)*

Below you will find weeks 27–31.

during	low	whole	reached	covered
today	however	happened	waves	space
across	best	black	remember	rock
ship	better	products	early	wind
top	short	hours	measure	listen

HIGH-FREQUENCY WORDS FLASH CARDS *(cont.)*

Below you will find weeks 32–36.

toward	vowel	numeral	map	seen
himself	passed	pattern	money	voice
hold	morning	against	slowly	draw
several	step	hundred	north	pulled
fast	five	true	table	farm

REFERENCES CITED

Fry, Edward. 2000. *1,000 Instant Words: The Most Common Words for Teaching Reading, Writing, and Spelling.* Huntington Beach, CA: Teacher Created Materials.

Marzano, Robert. 2010. "When Practice Makes Perfect...Sense." *Educational Leadership* 68 (3): 81–83.

McIntosh, Margaret E. 1997. "Formative Assessment in Mathematics." *The Clearing House: A Journal of Educational Strategies* 71 (2): 92–96.

US Department of Health and Human Services. 2000. *Report of the National Reading Panel: Teaching Children to Read: An Evidence-Based Assessment of the Scientific Research Literature on Reading and its Implications for Reading Instruction.* Washington, DC: US Government Printing Office.

CONTENTS OF THE DIGITAL RESOURCES

Teacher Resources

Resource	PDF Filename	Microsoft Word® Filename
Daily Descriptions	daily.pdf	daily.docx
Activity Descriptions	activity.pdf	activity.docx
Student Item Analysis Checklist	studentlog.pdf	studentlog.docx
Class Item Analysis	classlog.pdf	classlog.docx
Standards Chart	standards.pdf	

Student Resources

Resource	PDF Filename
BINGO Board	bingo.pdf
Word Board Game	boardgame.pdf
Word Bar Graph	wordgraph.pdf
Spinner	spinner.pdf
Tally It Up!	tally.pdf
Tiny Word Search	tinysearch.pdf
Ice Cream Sort	icecream.pdf
High-Frequency Words Flash Cards	flashcards.pdf

